Pearson's Canal Companion

OXFORD & GRAND UNION

Published by Central Waterways Supplies of Rugby - Tel/fax 01788 546692
email: sales@centralwaterways.co.uk Copyright: Michael Pearson - All rights reserved
Sixth edition 2006. ISBN 0 9549116 2 8   Printed by STIGE 10099 San Mauro, Turin, Italy

CW00677662

tillerman

Barely two years since the 5th edition marched proudly into London for the first time, the 6th edition of the *Oxford & Grand Union Canal Companion* follows hard on its heels, refining and updating its predecessor with contagious enthusiasm for some of the most characterful and culturally fascinating canals and river navigations in the country.

Sooner than imagined, it was nevertheless good to be back, boating on the crystal clear waters of the River Soar, cycling along the occasionally too bumpy for comfort Oxford Canal, or walking along stretches of the Grand Union Canal in Greater London where barges were once again plying commercially.

With the hospitality of David and Jennifer Alison the boating went smoothly, but cycling and walking not always so. A fair amount of money has been spent on upgrading towpaths in recent years, often by partnerships of local authorities, Sustrans and British Waterways aided by Government and European funding. This is all very laudable in itself, but the stakeholders need to remember that maintenance needs to be budgeted for as part of the package. Currently, lengths of both the Oxford and Grand Union canals, designated as long distance walking routes, leave something to be desired in terms of quality. It's like getting Charlie Dimmock in to give your garden a makeover, then shutting the gate for a couple of years and expecting everything to be rosy upon your return.

But don't let my churlish grouses deter you from following in my footsteps. Perhaps with greater use these towpaths will seem less overgrown in any case.

I thoroughly enjoyed revisiting these routes and I trust that you will too.

Michael Pearson

Market Harborough

UK-BOATING*holidays*

f you are looking for boating holiday you eed look no further

Hire direct from the leading narrowboat operators with all boats inspected and awarded star ratings by Visit Britain.

fleet of over 180 boats for 2 to 12 people om 11 start bases throughout the UK so u can be sure of the widest choice.

ginners are welcome

isit our website or telephone r a free brochure pack.

08701 217 670

www.uk-boating.com

The Oxford Canal

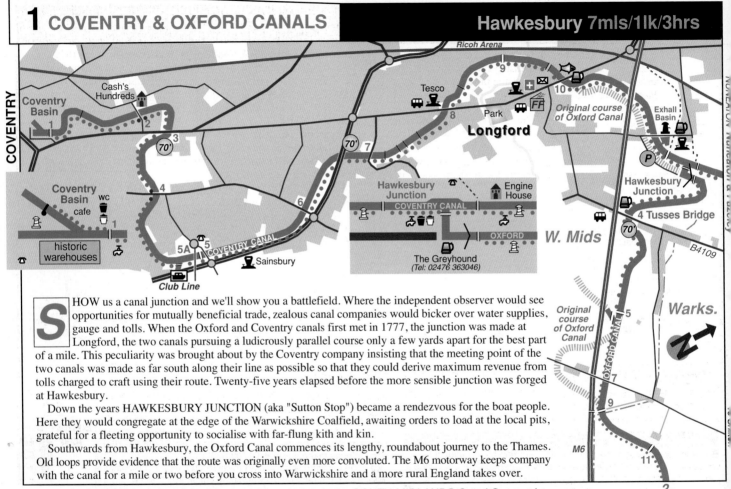

COVENTRY

Ricoh Arena

Coventry Basin

Cash's Hundreds

Tesco

Park

Longford

9

10

8

Original course of Oxford Canal

Exhall Basin

70'

70'

7

6

Coventry Basin

wc

cafe

1

historic warehouses

5A 5

COVENTRY CANAL

Sainsbury

Club Line

Hawkesbury Junction

COVENTRY CANAL

Engine House

OXFORD

The Greyhound
(Tel: 02476 363046)

W. Mids

Hawkesbury Junction

4 Tusses Bridge

70'

B4109

Warks.

Original course of Oxford Canal

5

OXFORD CANAL

7

9

M6

11

2

SHOW us a canal junction and we'll show you a battlefield. Where the independent observer would see opportunities for mutually beneficial trade, zealous canal companies would bicker over water supplies, gauge and tolls. When the Oxford and Coventry canals first met in 1777, the junction was made at Longford, the two canals pursuing a ludicrously parallel course only a few yards apart for the best part of a mile. This peculiarity was brought about by the Coventry company insisting that the meeting point of the two canals was made as far south along their line as possible so that they could derive maximum revenue from tolls charged to craft using their route. Twenty-five years elapsed before the more sensible junction was forged at Hawkesbury.

Down the years HAWKESBURY JUNCTION (aka "Sutton Stop") became a rendezvous for the boat people. Here they would congregate at the edge of the Warwickshire Coalfield, awaiting orders to load at the local pits, grateful for a fleeting opportunity to socialise with far-flung kith and kin.

Southwards from Hawkesbury, the Oxford Canal commences its lengthy, roundabout journey to the Thames. Old loops provide evidence that the route was originally even more convoluted. The M6 motorway keeps company with the canal for a mile or two before you cross into Warwickshire and a more rural England takes over.

A more detailed coverage of the Coventry Arm appears in the SOUTH MIDLANDS Canal Companion

T HE Oxford Canal slices through the grain of the countryside like someone cutting an appetising slice of fruit pie. But instead of oozing blackberry and apple filling, a rural landscape of shallow valleys and modest rises is exposed.

Canal and railway share an embankment near Brinklow, scene of many well known photographs and paintings depicting narrowboats and steam trains in quaint juxtaposition; tortoise and hare of 19th century transport. This, however, was not the original course of the canal. Reference to the map will indicate just how tortuous that once was. The embankments and cuttings that characterise the northern section of the Oxford now date from 'shortenings', undertaken between 1829 and 1834, which eliminated no less than fifteen miles between Hawkesbury and Braunston. As surveyed, Brindley's original route stretched the fifteen crow miles between Coventry and Napton into a staggering forty-three miles of convoluted canal. Brindley didn't care. He felt that the more places his canal visited, the more influence and commerce one might accrue. No-one expected canal transport to be fast. Its benefits lay in convenience and reliability. Even after the improvements old sections remained in use serving businesses and wharves already established on their banks.

STRETTON STOP was formerly a point at which tolls were taken. The scene here today is invariably busy and colourful. The old arm to Stretton Wharf is used for private moorings. Boaters should take care not to collide with the foot swing-bridge which links the towpath side with the boatbuilding sheds on the opposite bank.

Fosse Way crosses the canal at Bridge 30.

Map

CREWE
Hopsford Hall
hotel
golf course
18 19
17
M69
Ansty
Rose & Castle
16
14
15
13
13A
1
12
Former course of Oxford Canal
24
Nettle Hill
M6
Coombe Fields
26 27
Stretton Stop
28
29 30
Rose N'boats
A427 to Lutterworth
RUGBY
3
Fosse Way
Smite Brook
site of canal wharf
Brink-low

Ansty

ROSE & CASTLE - adjacent Bridge 15. Tel: 024 7661 2822. Vaguely canal-themed roadside pub with large garden spilling down to the canal. Extensive menu. *Buses into Coventry.*

Brinklow

Brinklow's agreeably wide main street is framed by an enjoyable miscellany of building styles and periods. At the edge of the village a pair of iron gates denote the location of a former wharf which lay on the old route of the canal. Past the Perpendicular church a lane leads up to the motte & bailey outline of a Norman castle. Thus Brinklow is altogether one of the best villages to visit along the 'northern' section of the Oxford Canal, but do *beware* of the Fosse Way traffic which moves much faster than the Romans ever envisaged.

WHITE LION - village centre. Tel: 01788 832579. Traditional country inn fronting on to village street, serving Banks's beer and offering food and accommodation. The village also boasts three other pubs, a fish & chip shop (Tel: 01788 832766) and Chinese takeaway (Tel: 01788 833257).

The boatyard shop stocks provisions, but also in the village, about ten minutes walk from the canal, you'll find a newsagent, post office and general store combined, as well as one or two antique shops. *Buses to Rugby.*

PROBABLY at its prettiest, the 'Northern Oxford' moves languidly from bridge-hole to bridge-hole in no apparent rush to get to Rugby, or anywhere else for that matter. And herein lies perhaps the greatest secret of canal travel: by removing the 'aims' and 'targets' with which we are apt to litter our highly stressed lives, a calmer, stress-free existence emerges, enabling all us inland waterway Houdinis to escape our self-imposed chains and bounds more effectively than those slaves to sun tans on Spanish beaches.

Bridge 32 carries the 'modernised', mid-nineteenth century towpath over the original route, retained as an arm to serve Brinklow. The depth of the 'new' cutting is considerable. It was the work of fledgling engineers Cubitt and Vignoles, both of whom were to make their reputations during the railway era.

At intervals, other sections of the original route join and leave the canal beneath the spans of elegant cast-iron bridges made by the Horseley Iron Works Company of Tipton whose structures proliferate on the BCN. These reedy old arms are, alas, no longer remotely navigable; a shame, they would have made delightful mooring backwaters of considerably more charm than the massive lagoons which have appeared all over the system. Their towpaths have vanished as well, rendering them unexplorable even on foot, though here and there an ancient bridge remains stranded surreally in the midst of some field or other.

At Newbold those with an enthusiasm for such things can discover one of the bricked up portals of the original tunnel at the edge of St Botolph's churchyard. This change of route explains why the "Boat Inn" seems to have nothing to do with the canal whereas it once fronted on to it. The Newbold Arm was kept profitably in water longer than most because it supplied the water troughs on the adjoining railway used by express steam trains to fill their tenders without stopping.

Map:

31 "Brinklow Arches"
32 Brinklow Arm
Brinklow
motte & bailey
34
35
36 37
38
39
41
42
Former course of Oxford Canal (Fennis Field Arm)
Footpath to Easenhall
sewage plant
43
Trent Valley Railway London - 86 miles
44 45
T.F. Yates 48
NEWBOLD TUNNEL
250 yards
old tunnel
Former course of Oxford Canal (Newbold Arm)
50
51
R. Avon

Newbold-on-Avon

With its church, canal wharf, and access to the infant River Avon, Newbold is a pleasant enough suburb of Rugby - useful for the replenishment of stores and some morale-boosting refreshment at one or other of the two pubs.

Adjacent to Newbold Tunnel, THE BOAT (Tel: 01788 576995) and BARLEY MOW (Tel: 01788 544174) compete for canal trade. There is also a fish & chip shop in Newbold. Alternatively, build up an appetite by walking across the fields from Bridge 37 to the pretty village of Easenhall.

It will take perhaps twenty minutes but the GOLDEN LION (Tel: 01788 832265) is a lovely country inn which makes it well worthwhile.

Large ALLDAYS store incorporating newagency, post office and cash machine plus a 'high class' butcher's shop.

BUSES - frequent weekday service to/from Rugby town centre and Hillmorton, the latter destination being useful for one-way towpath walks. Tel: 01788 535555.

THE saving in distance achieved by the 19th century improvements to the Oxford Canal is nowhere more apparent than in the vicinity of Rugby. In order to keep to the 300ft contour and minimise earthworks, the original route went wandering off a couple of miles to the north, looking for a convenient point to cross the River Swift. Then, having returned to the outskirts of Rugby via Brownsover, it set off again, this time to cross the River Avon near Clifton-on-Dunsmore. Paid by the mile, the contractors must have laughed all the way to the bank.

The outskirts of Rugby are not especially pretty, but neither are they dull. Retail parks, ring roads, industrial units, housing estates and all the other accumulated junk of modern day life are paraded for the canal traveller's contempt. Cubitt's new route involved a sequence of aqueducts and embankments across the wide valleys of the Swift and Avon which form a confluence just to the south. It makes for a fascinating journey to this day, conifers masking the proximity of factories and shops, and there is barely a dull moment as the entrances and exits of the old loops are passed, and you try to do a Sherlock Holmes on the topography of the original canal. A footpath leads enticingly along the old Brownsover Arm. There are lost railways to decipher as well. The Midland, London & North Western and Great Central all converged on Rugby, all crossed the canal, and all fell foul of Beeching. The Stamford and Peterborough line left Rugby on a high, curving viaduct which still looms poignantly over the local golf course.

By road, Rugby and Hillmorton are inseparable. The canal, though, takes its time in travelling between the two, dallying in the fields before a widening, fringed by reed beds, heralds the first of three duplicated locks carrying the canal up past the Oxford Canal Company's dignified workshops, framed by Bridge 70. British Waterways have developed a complex of small business units here.

Hillmorton's canalscape has a backdrop of wireless masts - a dozen of the tallest being 820ft high - of necessity lit red at night to ward off low-flying aircraft. Rugby Radio Station dates from 1926 and was used to operate the first trans-Atlantic radio telephone link between London and New York. Nowadays the station transmits telecommunications all over the world and also broadcasts time signals on behalf of the Royal Observatory with an accuracy of one second in three thousand years.

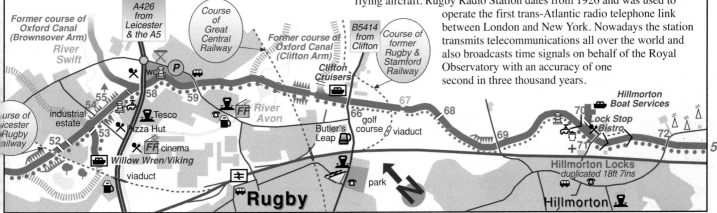

The off-puttting fact that the centre of Rugby is such a trek from the canal is no excuse for not taking the trouble to visit this interesting and occasionally not unhandsome market town. Rugby's reputation is inextricably linked with its famous public school. Founded in 1567, it wasn't until its best known headmaster, Dr Arnold, arrived on the scene in 1828 that the glory years ensued. Ever since, Rugby has held its place among the top schools in the country, and a steady stream of former pupils have gone on to make their mark on the world. Ironically, it was a boy with possibly less than average intellect who made the greatest gesture of all when, one day in 1823, to alleviate the boredom of a football match, he picked up the ball and ran with it, thereby founding the game of 'rugby'. A plaque in the close adjacent to the school commemorates William Webb Ellis's defiant gesture, whilst nearby stands a statue to Thomas Hughes, former pupil and author of *Tom Brown's Schooldays*. Rugby School's past roll-call is particularly rich in such literary figures, and includes Matthew Arnold (son of the headmaster), 'Lewis Carroll', Walter Savage Landor and Rupert Brooke.

HARVESTER INN - canalside Bridge 58. Plus Holiday Express hotel. Tel: 01788 569466.

BUTLER'S LEAP - 5 minutes walk south-west of Bridge 66. Brewers Fayre family pub. Tel: 01788 577650. *There are now internet cafe and laundry facilities nearby at Clifton Cruisers.*

LOCK STOP BISTRO - canalside at Hillmorton. Tel: 01788 553562. Breakfasts, lunches and dinners in bistro beside the canal - closed Mondays and Tuesdays.

ASK - High Street. Contemporary Italian. Tel: 01788 553220.

SUMMERSAULT - High Street, town centre. Recently extended award winning restaurant and coffee house housed in shop also dealing in crafts and clothing. Tel: 01788 543223.

LA MARGHERITA - Church Street. Mediterranean restaurant. Tel: 01788 550289.

BARBY SPORTING CLUB - access via Bridge 76, Map 5. Restaurant food. Tel: 01788 891873.

All facilities are to be found in the town centre just over a mile south of Bridge 59 (from where there are frequent local buses). Rugby is a comprehensive shopping centre without being overpowering, and in addition to the standard chain stores there are a fair number of long established local retailers. Outdoor markets are held on Mondays, Fridays and Saturdays.

TOURIST INFORMATION - Rugby Art Gallery and Museum. Tel: 01788 534970.

RUGBY ART GALLERY & MUSEUM - Little Elborow Street. Rugby's latest cultural attraction, featuring modern British art, the Tripontium Collection of Roman artifacts and social history objects relating to the town. Tel: 01788 533201.

RUGBY SCHOOL MUSEUM - Little Church Street. Tel: 01788 556109. Museum open Mon-Sat with guided tours at 2.30pm.

RUGBY FOOTBALL MUSEUM - St Matthews Street. Place of pilgrimage for lovers of the oval ball game. Open Mon-Sat, 9am-5pm, admission free. Tel: 01788 567777.

BUSES - services throughout the area - Tel: 01788 535555.

TRAINS - station half a mile south of Bridge 59. Tel: 08457 484950.

TAXIS - People Express. Tel: 01788 565888.

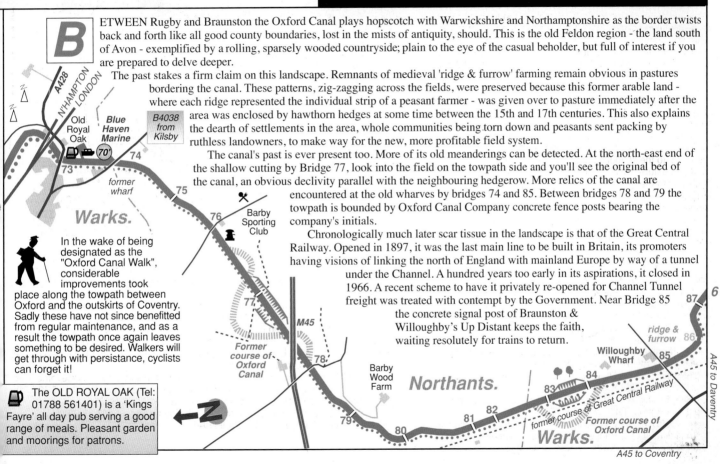

BETWEEN Rugby and Braunston the Oxford Canal plays hopscotch with Warwickshire and Northamptonshire as the border twists back and forth like all good county boundaries, lost in the mists of antiquity, should. This is the old Feldon region - the land south of Avon - exemplified by a rolling, sparsely wooded countryside; plain to the eye of the casual beholder, but full of interest if you are prepared to delve deeper.

The past stakes a firm claim on this landscape. Remnants of medieval 'ridge & furrow' farming remain obvious in pastures bordering the canal. These patterns, zig-zagging across the fields, were preserved because this former arable land - where each ridge represented the individual strip of a peasant farmer - was given over to pasture immediately after the area was enclosed by hawthorn hedges at some time between the 15th and 17th centuries. This also explains the dearth of settlements in the area, whole communities being torn down and peasants sent packing by ruthless landowners, to make way for the new, more profitable field system.

The canal's past is ever present too. More of its old meanderings can be detected. At the north-east end of the shallow cutting by Bridge 77, look into the field on the towpath side and you'll see the original bed of the canal, an obvious declivity parallel with the neighbouring hedgerow. More relics of the canal are encountered at the old wharves by bridges 74 and 85. Between bridges 78 and 79 the towpath is bounded by Oxford Canal Company concrete fence posts bearing the company's initials.

Chronologically much later scar tissue in the landscape is that of the Great Central Railway. Opened in 1897, it was the last main line to be built in Britain, its promoters having visions of linking the north of England with mainland Europe by way of a tunnel under the Channel. A hundred years too early in its aspirations, it closed in 1966. A recent scheme to have it privately re-opened for Channel Tunnel freight was treated with contempt by the Government. Near Bridge 85 the concrete signal post of Braunston & Willoughby's Up Distant keeps the faith, waiting resolutely for trains to return.

In the wake of being designated as the "Oxford Canal Walk", considerable improvements took place along the towpath between Oxford and the outskirts of Coventry. Sadly these have not since benefitted from regular maintenance, and as a result the towpath once again leaves something to be desired. Walkers will get through with persistance, cyclists can forget it!

The OLD ROYAL OAK (Tel: 01788 561401) is a 'Kings Fayre' all day pub serving a good range of meals. Pleasant garden and moorings for patrons.

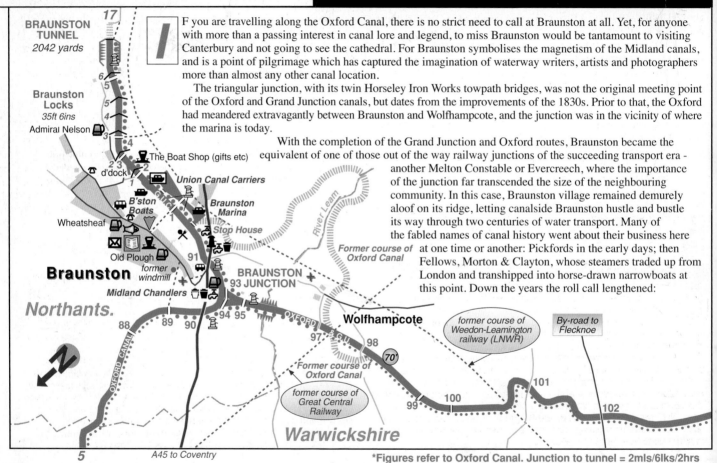

IF you are travelling along the Oxford Canal, there is no strict need to call at Braunston at all. Yet, for anyone with more than a passing interest in canal lore and legend, to miss Braunston would be tantamount to visiting Canterbury and not going to see the cathedral. For Braunston symbolises the magnetism of the Midland canals, and is a point of pilgrimage which has captured the imagination of waterway writers, artists and photographers more than almost any other canal location.

The triangular junction, with its twin Horseley Iron Works towpath bridges, was not the original meeting point of the Oxford and Grand Junction canals, but dates from the improvements of the 1830s. Prior to that, the Oxford had meandered extravagantly between Braunston and Wolfhampcote, and the junction was in the vicinity of where the marina is today.

With the completion of the Grand Junction and Oxford routes, Braunston became the equivalent of one of those out of the way railway junctions of the succeeding transport era - another Melton Constable or Evercreech, where the importance of the junction far transcended the size of the neighbouring community. In this case, Braunston village remained demurely aloof on its ridge, letting canalside Braunston hustle and bustle its way through two centuries of water transport. Many of the fabled names of canal history went about their business here at one time or another: Pickfords in the early days; then Fellows, Morton & Clayton, whose steamers traded up from London and transhipped into horse-drawn narrowboats at this point. Down the years the roll call lengthened:

Map labels:

BRAUNSTON TUNNEL 2042 yards
Braunston Locks 35ft 6ins
Admiral Nelson
The Boat Shop (gifts etc)
d'dock
Union Canal Carriers
B'ston Boats
Braunston Marina
Wheatsheaf
Stop House
Old Plough
former windmill
Braunston
Midland Chandlers
Northants.
BRAUNSTON JUNCTION
Former course of Oxford Canal
Wolfhampcote
former course of Weedon-Leamington railway (LNWR)
By-road to Flecknoe
Former course of Oxford Canal
former course of Great Central Railway
OXFORD CANAL
Warwickshire
A45 to Coventry

*Figures refer to Oxford Canal. Junction to tunnel = 2mls/6lks/2hrs

Nursers, boatbuilders, and painters of arguably the most sublime 'Roses & Castles' ever seen on the system; Samuel Barlow, the coal carriers whose boats were always in the most pristine of condition; and, towards the end, Willow Wren and Blue Line, who kept canal carrying defiantly afloat into the era of the juggernaut.

But the working boats have gone, and with them, inevitably, something of Braunston's old magic. Nevertheless, this is still a flourishing canal centre, home to a hire fleet and a massive marina based on former reservoirs, as well as numerous canal-based industries from boatbuilders to suppliers of traditional boater's wear. Wander along the towpath and you'll see new boats being built, old ones restored, and a regular stream of traffic up and down the locks, and it only takes the aroma of a charcoal stove, the beat of a Bolinder, or the rattle of the ratchets in the twilight of an autumn afternoon for the old days to be evoked, making you glad you came.

Not without controversy, the former 'Stop House' has ceased serving as a British Waterways office - institutionally prone to change, BW have decamped to a business park in Milton Keynes - but a skeleton information service remains on certain pre-designated days. Six wide beam locks carry the Grand Union up to the mouth of Braunston Tunnel. Water and energy can be saved by working through them in company. Passage in under an hour is eminently possible given sufficient enthusiasm. Braunston Tunnel takes about twenty minutes to negotiate. What happens at the other end is detailed on Map 17.

The five mile section between Braunston and Napton is interesting scenically and historically. It is a thoroughly remote length of canal; the countryside falling flatly away to the north-west, but climbing abruptly to a notable ridge in the opposite direction. There are ghosts and echoes everywhere: reedy old loops; abandoned railways; lost villages; and, at Wolfhampcote, a 'friendless church'.

When the Grand Union Canal was formed in 1929, there remained a gap between its former Grand Junction (London-Braunston) and Warwick & Napton constituents which belonged to the Oxford Canal. Knowing a good thing when they saw it, the Oxford company kindly allowed the Grand Union to pick up the tab for a programme of dredging and concrete banking, at the same time continuing to extract tolls from them until Nationalisation. A phenomenon relating to this 'joint' length is that boats travelling between the Midlands and the South, via either the Oxford or the Grand Union, pass each other going in the opposite direction; shades of the Great Western and Southern railways at Exeter, or the GWR and LMS at Chester.

Braunston

Village Braunston straddles its ridge, four hundred feet up on the slopes of the Northamptonshire uplands. Enclosed fields, still bearing the pattern of ridge & furrow, distil the spirit of the Middle Ages. Sauntering along the High Street from the village green to the tall spired church, one encounters a mixture of stone and brick buildings, including a sail-less and now residential windmill and a 17th century manor house.

At the foot of a long hill the A45 crosses the canal. This was the Chester turnpike road which became part of Telford's route from London to Holyhead. Now, handsome modern flats overlook the marina, and Braunston must be as busy and as populated as never before, though it still contrives to evoke a timeless air which has much to commend it.

THE MILL HOUSE - canalside Bridge 91. Family pub and carvery with customer moorings and children's garden; also accommodation and day boat hire. Tel: 01788 890450.

THE OLD PLOUGH - High Street. One of two village locals. Tel: 01788 890000.
THE WHEATSHEAF - village centre. Tel: 01788 890748.
ADMIRAL NELSON - canalside Bridge 4. Popular, refurbished canalside inn. Restaurant and bar meals, attractive garden. Tel: 01788 890075.
Fish & chips in the village open Wed-Sat evenings and Fri & Sat lunchtimes - Tel: 01788 890258. Floating cafe by the Stop House.

Facilities include a LONDIS general store and post office (who advertise that they are happy to deliver to your boat - Tel: 01788 890334), an enterprising butcher who makes his own chutneys and sauces, and a Christian bookshop and tea room. Down by the canal, by the bottom lock, THE BOAT SHOP opens from 8am-8pm throughout the summer season and deals in just about everything from gifts to groceries.

BUSES - Geoff Amos Coaches to/from Rugby and Banbury. Tel: 01327 260522. Mon-Sat service, useful for towpath walks.

AT Napton Junction (known to working boatmen as Wigrams Turn) the Oxford Canal sets off southwards on its long, winding road to the Thames. Despite the proximity of two busy marinas, the junction itself is typically remote. A 1930s concrete bridge spans the entrance and exit of the Grand Union route, formerly the Warwick & Napton Canal. Interestingly, it is numbered 17. Where (we can hear you wondering) are the other sixteen? The answer is that they were in the Grand Union Company's imagination. When they acquired rights to the route from Braunston to Birmingham in 1929 they re-numbered the sequence of bridges from Braunston northwards, including those on the Oxford Canal as far as Napton which never actually bore the GU numbers allocated to them.

East of Napton the shared section of the Oxford and Grand Union routes pursues its lonely course, passing the small settlement of Lower Shuckburgh and its picturesque Victorian church. A footpath climbs from here through parkland to the medieval village of Upper Shuckburgh. The name is said to mean 'a hill haunted by goblins'. Certainly Beacon Hill, rising to 678 feet, has its spirits. A 17th century member of the Shuckburgh family is said to have been accosted by King Charles I whilst hunting on the hill. The King, on his way to fight at the Battle of Edgehill, demanded to know how an English gentleman could spare time for hunting when his King was fighting for his crown.

Whilst the Grand Union heads determinedly off towards Birmingham, the more poetically minded Oxford picks its way quietly around the skirts of Napton Hill, a gentle summit half eaten away by old quarry workings. For the best part of a century clay was extracted from the hill and used in the manufacture of bricks at the works by Bridge 112. Narrowboats carried the finished products to Napton railway station on the Warwick & Napton Canal a couple of miles north of Napton Junction. Nowadays the site of the works is occupied by various light industries.

NAPTON LOCKS lift the canal up to the hamlet of Marston Doles. With a

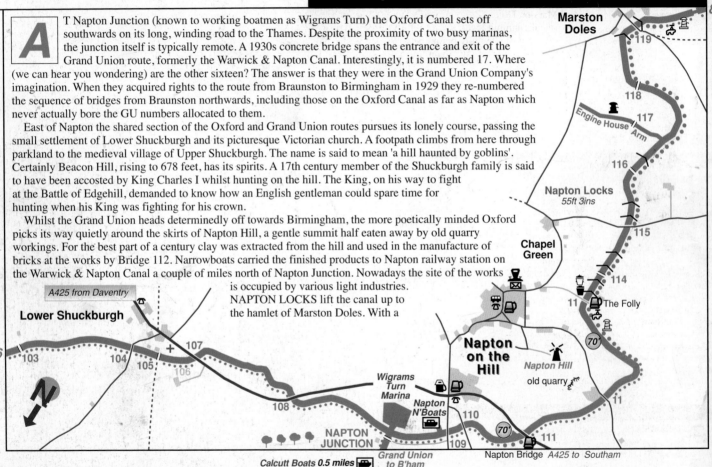

well-surfaced towpath and a lock-wheeling lock-keeper (at busy times at any rate) the flight seems a snip; though at the height of summer there may be queues. The 'Napton and Marston Doles Backpumping Scheme' has improved water supply to the canal's summit level. Napton's famous windmill is a constant landmark, whilst in the lengthy pound between the top two locks and the rest a branch canal leaves the main line and appears to head off across the fields towards Beacon Hill. This is the Engine House Arm, dug to enable boats to bring coal to a stationary steam engine which once pumped water through a system of channels and pipes back to the summit section; the arm is now in use as a backwater for linear moorings. The top lock is overlooked by a handsome, trapezium-shaped warehouse, nowadays in use as offices.

Napton on the Hill

Napton (best reached from Bridge 113) basks in the sunshine (and occasionally gales) on its south-facing hill. Its street pattern takes some fathoming, but there is much green space between the houses and even the seemingly obligatory modern developments dovetail neatly into the whole. You can climb towards the windmill for a better view, but it is never open to the public.

THE BRIDGE AT NAPTON - canalside Bridge 111. Bar & restaurant meals and pleasant garden. Tel: 01926 812466.
THE FOLLY - adjacent Bridge 113. Long ago known as "The Bull & Butcher", and relicensed after many dry years in 1990. Tel: 01926 815185.
KING'S HEAD - on A425 south of Bridge 109. Food and Hook Norton, a heady mixture. Tel: 01926 812202.

Napton lies half a mile east of Bridge 113 with a vibrant post office stores (who are happy to deliver orders to your boat - Tel: 01926 812488) catering for most requirements, including freshly baked bread. The Folly Canal Shop, adjacent to the pub, sells basic provisions and souvenirs.

BUSES - useful links with Leamington Spa for towpath walkers. Tel: 0870 608 2 608.

Fenny Compton Wharf *(Map 8)*

THE WHARF - canalside Bridge 136. Revitalised canalside inn offering excellent food in comfortable surroundings. Tel: 01295 770332. Large canalside garden. Adnams admirable ales from Suffolk.

Meadowsweet on the Oxford Summit

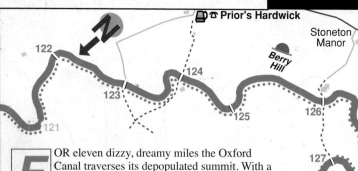

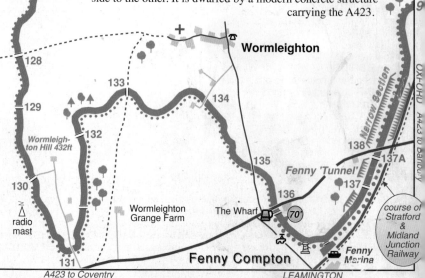

Prior's Hardwick

Stoneton Manor

Berry Hill

122
124
123
125
126
121
7
127
128
129
132
Wormleigh-ton Hill 432ft
130
131
radio mast
133
134
135
136
137A
137
138
Wormleighton
Wormleighton Grange Farm
The Wharf
70'
Fenny 'Tunnel'
Fenny Marina
Fenny Compton
Narrow Section
OXf-OHU A423 to Banbury
9
course of Stratford & Midland Junction Railway
A423 to Coventry
LEAMINGTON

FOR eleven dizzy, dreamy miles the Oxford Canal traverses its depopulated summit. With a compass, a pair of stout walking shoes and a healthy disregard for the laws of trespass, you could do it in four. But because - as the poet Edward Thomas put it - "there is nothing at the end of any road better than can be found beside it" - you feel no desire to count the miles, no temptation to begrudge Brindley his watershed wanderings.

We used to say that the Oxford's summit was as shallow as a matinee idol's smile, but dredging in recent years has increased the depth of water available and it is now perfectly feasible to average something in the region of three miles an hour. If only the towpath was equally well-maintained. Considering its status as a designated walk, little attempt appears to be made to keep the rampant vegetation in check; budgetary limitations one imagines.

The loneliness of the summit has a mystic, trance-inducing quality. Grazing flocks of sheep are your only neighbours. Your soliloquies meet with their unconcealed disdain. From time to time you may catch glimpses of another boat on what has every appearance of a parallel running waterway, and you take some convincing before accepting that this is really a boat ahead of you, or behind you, on the same convoluted canal. Shades of the Leeds & Liverpool Canal's Marton Pool which evokes equal disorientations.

Wormleighton sleeps the sleep of the innocent on a gentle slope overlooking the canal's meanderings. Chief delight is the gatehouse dating from 1613, built from local stone the colour of a weatherbeaten face. South of the wharf at Fenny Compton (see page 15) the canal negotiates a deep, narrow cutting. When the canal was first built there was a thousand yard tunnel here. But the rock was brittle and the bore a bottleneck, and in time the top was taken off. Bridge 137A is an elegant cast iron turnover bridge carrying the towpath from one side to the other. It is dwarfed by a modern concrete structure carrying the A423.

SOUTHBOUND, the Oxford begins its long, drawn out descent to the Thames. Northwards, CLAYDON marks the start of the summit section; no more locks to work for four or five hours! Wormleighton, Boddington and Clattercote are not, as you might assume, a firm of Banbury solicitors, but rather the three reservoirs which feed the Oxford Canal. Water shortages have always been a problem on this waterway and at times the density of pleasure traffic exacerbates the situation.

Bridge 141 straddles the county boundary and is the northernmost of the characteristic draw bridges synonymous with this canal. They are simplicity defined, consisting of no more than a pair of shallow brick abutments, a platform and two hefty timber balance beams set at 45 degrees when the bridge is closed to boats, or flat against the nettles when, as is often the case, they are left open. Seen from afar, they punctuate the Oxford Canal's passage through the Cherwell Valley, as homogeneous with this landscape as the pollarded willows of its watermeadows and the oolite stonework of its villages.

The course of the old Stratford & Midland Junction Railway parallels the canal by Bridge 142 which spans the feeder from Boddington Reservoir. The railway was one of those forgotten little lines whose high hopes were never realised. It became disparagingly, but affectionately known as the 'Slow, Mouldy and Jolting'. L.T.C. Rolt loved the unhurried progress of its trains, their "slow, panting climbs, and swift, swaying descents" across the Northamptonshire uplands. Brian Collings, our cover artist, travelled on the line's last passenger train in 1952 - see also Map 20.

At CLAYDON TOP LOCK, the Oxford Canal Company built workshops and stables. This would have been a busy spot in the heyday of the canal. Three isolated locks interrupt the canal's otherwise uneventful progress between Claydon and Cropredy. At CROPREDY the canal itself narrows by the old toll office and manager's house, whilst south of Bridge 153 a former coal wharf provides room to turn a seventy footer. Visitor moorings are provided north of Cropredy Lock, a pleasant base from which to savour the delights of this lovely village.

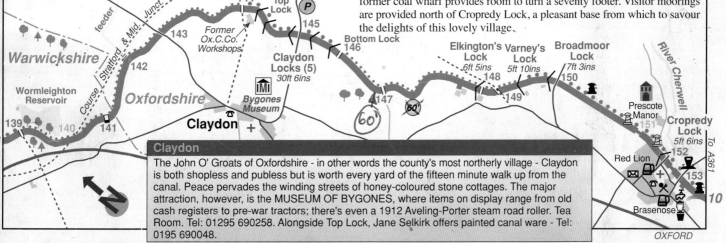

Claydon

The John O' Groats of Oxfordshire - in other words the county's most northerly village - Claydon is both shopless and publess but is worth every yard of the fifteen minute walk up from the canal. Peace pervades the winding streets of honey-coloured stone cottages. The major attraction, however, is the MUSEUM OF BYGONES, where items on display range from old cash registers to pre-war tractors; there's even a 1912 Aveling-Porter steam road roller. Tea Room. Tel: 01295 690258. Alongside Top Lock, Jane Selkirk offers painted canal ware - Tel: 0195 690048.

Cropredy *(Map 9)*

Cropredy is the village with the closest relationship to the Oxford Canal and, as such, makes an ideal place to break your journey, whether on foot or afloat. In recent years it has become famous in folk music circles as the location of an annual (August) festival centred round the enduring folk rock group *Fairport Convention*. But this is one music festival where locals and visitors seem in harmony: the Brasenose Inn even features on the cover of one of Fairport's albums.

You have to go back over three hundred years to the other most significant event in Cropredy's mellow existence. There was a Civil War battle here in 1644. Ten thousand men took part and some of the clobber they left behind - helmets, bayonets and cannon balls - is on display in the church, along with a pre-Reformation brass lectern which was apparently submerged in the Cherwell to keep it safe from the marauding Puritans.

THE RED LION - adjacent Bridge 152. Thatched village inn visited by Temple Thurston (*The Flower of Gloster*) and L.T.C. Rolt (*Narrow Boat*). It has lost none of its charm. Sunbeams still slant through the neighbouring churchyard and glint on your pint. Good range of food usually available. Families welcome. Tel: 01295 750224.

THE BRASENOSE INN - 300 yards west of Bridge 153. Classic country local offering bar and restaurant meals. Tel: 01295 750244.

THE GREEN SCENE - Cropredy Green. Coffees, light lunches and afternoon teas in the enjoyable surroundings of a small craft shop. Tables spill idyllically out on to the pavement on warm days. Tel: 01295 758085.

BRIDGE STORES by Bridge 153 is open daily stocking groceries, wines & spirits, newspapers, gifts, cash machine and Calor gas. Deeper into the village you'll come across a post office and the charming 'Green Scene' gallery and coffee shop.

BUSES - infrequent (but useful for one way towpath walks) service connects with Banbury. Tel: 0870 608 2 608.

Banbury *(Map 10)*

Once an Oxfordshire market town, now seemingly an extension of London's commuterland, Banbury is a useful place for shopping, replenishing the wallet and stocking up on tourist literature at the excellent TIC. Since construction of the M40, Banbury has brightened-up its act and takes more pride in its appearance than the world-weary, traffic-blighted place it used to be. The streets are cleaner and more revealing of the pleasant architecture surviving from its heyday as a bustling country town. Our favourite building is the former corn merchants by the market place, its upper storey a signwritten reminder of Banbury's importance as an agricultural centre. Neither has the town forgotten its niche in the pantheon of nursery rhymes, and a replica cross (erected by the Victorians following removal of the original by a Puritan mob in 1600) can still be seen at the southern end of The Horsefair.

CHURCH HOUSE - North Bar. Tel: 01295 265466. Stylish bar and restaurant up at the far end of town from the canal.

CAFE QUAY - canalside. Tel: 01295 270444. Light and airy modern licensed eating place. Coffees, teas, lunches.

THAI ORCHID - North Bar. Tel: 01295 270833. Flamboyant ethnic restaurant and take-away.

YE OLDE REINDEER INN - Parsons Street. Tel: 01295 264031. Banbury's oldest inn dating from 1570. Hook Norton ales.

BANESBERIE'S - Butchers Row. Tel: 01295 269066. Coffees, lunches and teas with Banbury cakes.

FABIO'S - North Bar. Tel: 01925 250507. Lively Italian restaurant.

ROSAMUND THE FAIR - cruising restaurant offering public trips on Saturday evenings and Sunday lunchtimes. Tel: 01295 278690.

The canalside CASTLE QUAY shopping centre likes to think that it has put upstart Milton Keynes in its place, but, better still, is the lively Farmer's Market held on the first Friday of each month. Certainly as far as canal travellers are concerned there's no excuse for not laying in stores.

MUSEUM & TOURIST INFORMATION - canalside. Tel: 01295 259855. An impressive new development celebrating varying aspects of the town's past with emphasis on the canal. Open daily, admission free.

TOOLEY'S BOATYARD - canalside. Tel: 01295 272917. Gifts, chandlery, boat trips and day boat hire.

BUSES - services throughout the area. Tel: 0870 608 2 608.

TRAINS - Chiltern, Thames and Virgin services to/from Oxford, Leamington, London & Birmingham.
Tel: 08457 484950.

TAXIS - A1 Taxis. Tel: 01295 278690.

AT Cropredy the Oxford Canal makes eye contact with the River Cherwell, but like all good bodice-rippers, the affair takes many twists and turns before consumation takes place. The canal company purchased Cropredy Mill and adapted the mill stream to provide the canal with water. Slat Mill, wherever it stood, whatever it ground, has long gone. With the river and railway as companions, the canal progresses uneventfully through a rural landscape. By Hardwick Lock the M40 motorway makes its northernmost crossing of the canal. Below the lock, and overlooked by a large aluminium plant, the canal parallels the course of the Oxfordshire Ironstone Railway built by German prisoners of the First World War to access the ironstone quarries west of Banbury. Part of its trackbed, along with several miles of towpath, is included in the "Banbury Fringe Circular Walk".

Banbury sits like a bad bruise on the peaches and cream complexion of the Oxford Canal. For two or three turgid miles the picturesque images usually associated with this canal are invaded by ring-roads, factories and urban sprawl. But paradoxically, one can't help but feel grateful for a change of scene: all those meadows and wooded ridges can be a bit unremitting when encountered at three miles an hour.

Banbury was the location, in 1955, of a campaigning boat rally to fight proposals to abandon the Oxford Canal. Seeing how busy the canal is now only serves to illustrate the folly of such short-sighted thinking. Trade on the Oxford Canal petered out towards the end of the 1950s. Amongst the last regular cargoes were timber and tar. Up until this time Banbury supported its own canal community who were wont to congregate at a spit and sawdust pub called The Struggler. L. T. C. Rolt immortalised it in his *Inland Waterways of England*. The pub and the canal wharf were demolished in 1962 by the local council, who added insult to injury by building a bus station on the site. Now the whole area has been redeveloped into the Castle Quay Shopping Centre and Rolt may well be looking down from heaven and chuckling - with irony. By all means commemorate the great man - but on a *road* bridge! At least Tooley's drydock, also made famous by Rolt as the scene of *Cressy's* docking and refitting prior to the cruise of 1939 recounted in *Narrow Boat*, is preserved as part of the excellent new Banbury Museum whose inland waterways gallery imaginatively spans the canal.

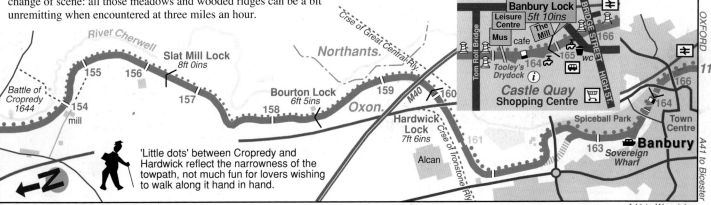

'Little dots' between Cropredy and Hardwick reflect the narrowness of the towpath, not much fun for lovers wishing to walk along it hand in hand.

By-road to Gt. Bourton   A423 to Coventry   A41 to Warwick

DRAW bridges abound, their functional looks disguising the economy of construction inherent in their design. Most of them will be chained 'open' and thus of no hindrance to boaters. Another worthwhile cost-cutting measure south of Banbury was the provision of single bottom gates for each lock chamber instead of the more usual mitred pairs.

The rocket-like spire of Kings Sutton church soars above the watermeadows, finding a photogenic mirror image in the canal from certain angles. The village boasts a railway station, but its other facilities are a bit of a hike away on the far side of the Cherwell, which forms the boundary between Oxon and Northants. A plume of smoke flumes from the fertilizer works at Twyford Mill.

Kings Sutton Lock is delightful. The keeper's cottage is simply built of brick with stone facing. On the opposite bank stands a former blacksmith's forge and stable block decorated by the addition of the village station's old name board. South of here the canal momentarily sheds its man-made character. The branches of pollarded willows hang caressingly over the water and poplars whisper in the breeze as a belt of woodland is encountered.

Into this exquisite landscape the M40 intrudes like a kick in the groin. When it was being constructed in the 1980s the *Sunday Times* ran a sequence of photographs looking out over the Cherwell Valley in the vicinity of Kings Sutton. It was a sobering illustration of the assassination of the Oxfordshire landscape. As hideous in its way as the sort of photographs they show of bodies in the streets after a military coup. As the Department of Transport used to boast, road schemes such as the M40 had their viability tested on a 'cost benefit basis'. Yes, we know: for the road lobby's benefit at the countryside's cost.

But how long before the motorway is outmoded like the canal itself and the now dismantled Banbury & Cheltenham Railway? The canal can be said to have functioned commercially for over a hundred and fifty years. The railway was relatively shortlived, opening in 1887 and closing to passengers in 1951, though surviving in goods use for another thirteen years. Its most celebrated train was the *Ports to Ports Express*, a service designed to effect the transfer of merchant seamen between Tyneside and South Wales. Did they, catching a glimpse of passing 'joshers', feel momentarily at home on their ten hour, landlocked journey?

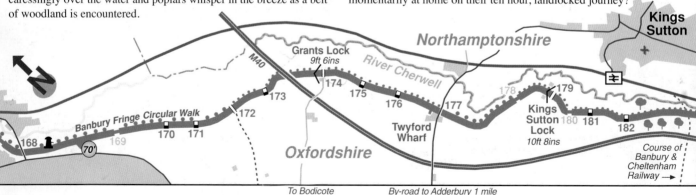

THE motorway bridge carries a dedication to a young civil engineering student fatally injured during construction of the road. Passing briefly into Northamptonshire, the canal shares much of this part of its journey with the adjoining railway, but loses little of its tranquillity in the process. Wharves past and present recall the canal's original purpose. The one at AYNHO remains remarkably intact, its brick warehouse being home to a shop selling canal souvenirs, confectionary and a modest range of provisions.

Aynho's long closed railway station is of Brunellian design, dating from the inception of the original mixed gauge line between Oxford and Birmingham. When the Great Western Railway shaved twenty miles off their London to Birmingham route in 1910, Aynho marked the northern end of the 'cut off'. The lofty viaducts of the new line (now revitalised by Chiltern Trains) form a handsome backdrop to the canal.

Having played coquettishly with the canal's affections since Cropredy, the Cherwell acquires carnal knowledge by Aynho Weir Lock as the channel flows directly across the canal. The lock itself is shallow and diamond-shaped, Somerton being so deep that extra capacity had to be built into Aynho.

SOMERTON DEEP LOCK is, well, *very* deep. Overlooked by an exceptionally pretty cottage (where ice creams are on sale) it vies with Tardebigge on the Worcester & Birmingham for the honour of being the deepest narrowbeam chamber on the canal system. Certainly the steerer's eye view of things, when the lock is empty, is reminiscent of an elephant trap. Heaven knows how single-handed boat captains managed in the past. Tom Foxon hinted at his methods in *Number One*, also relating how it was his habit to swap lumps of coal with the lock-keeper in exchange for fresh laid eggs and a rabbit or two.

Down Somerton way the towpath becomes more of a footpath, a pleasant change for walkers, but virtually impassible by cyclists.

Aynho Wharf

GREAT WESTERN ARMS - Aynho Wharf. Congenial pub located between the canal and the old railway station and suitably decorated with memorabilia relating to both modes of transport. A tad more sophisticated and food-orientated than of yore, perhaps, but welcoming and well-appointed and still dispensing heavenly Hook Norton ales. Tel: 01869 338288.

AYNHO WHARF - boatyard with shop selling gifts and groceries. Also snack bar dispensing tea, coffee etc.

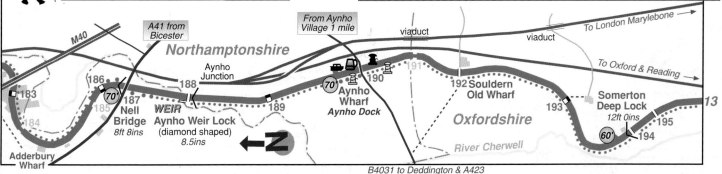

21

Somerton Deep Lock

CANAL, railway and river saunter along the valley floor, but the roads keep cautiously to the shoulders of the hills. When the Cherwell bursts its banks, the escaping water forms an inland sea and wildfowl find this an attractive wintering ground. In spring the meadows seem full of lapwings carrying out their dizzy courtship; later, the sky is still rewardingly filled with lark-song.

Between Somerton and Heyford the canal assumes the character of a river. The towpath loses its formality, becoming more of a track through the adjoining fields. Pollarded willows line the canal's banks, just as they do the Cherwell's, so that seen from a passing train, it is often difficult to tell immediately which is which.

Joni Mitchell's dream has come true - 'the bombers in the sky have turned to butterflies' - now that the giant American airbase at Upper Heyford has been mothballed. The absence of aircraft renders the Cherwell Valley uncannily quiet. Strange how the end of the Cold War should spread ripples to this peaceful corner of Oxfordshire.

Between the two Heyfords the canal arcs deliciously through a belt of woodland. There are glimpses of an attractive cluster of stone buildings - a church, manor house and 15th century tithe barn - below Allen's Lock. Lower Heyford Mill ceased working at the end of the Second World War. Lift-bridge No. 205 is said to have been built of iron to take the weight of the miller's traction engine.

HEYFORD WHARF is very similar to Aynho (Map 12), but on this occasion the warehouse is built of local stone. Nowadays it is in use as a hire base. Heyford railway station stands usefully alongside Bridge 206. A short walk from here lies Rousham House and its famous gardens, the work of William Kent. The gardens are open to the public all year round. The 17th century house is open to the public on Wednesday and Sunday afternoons between April and September, but children and dogs are frowned upon! William Kent's 'Rousham Eyecatcher' can be seen over the brow of the hill from Heyford Common lock.

Map labels: Somerton; 196; 60'; mill; 197; 198; 199; pipe; 200; 201; Heyford Common Lock 7ft 2ins; 202; 203; 204; Allen's Lock 5ft 0ins; Upper Heyford; River Cherwell; Footpath to Steeple Aston; mill 205; B4030; Lower Heyford; Oxfordshire Narrowboats; 60'; 206; 207; Heyford Wharf; The Cleeves; Rousham Park; 14

The Heyfords

THE BELL - Market Square, Lower Heyford. Picturesque, creeper-clad, stone-built inn overlooking the former market place. Adnams and Greene King ales, and a good choice of food from baguettes upwards. Garden and games. Tel: 01869 347176.
BARLEY MOW - Somerton Road, Upper Heyford. Access from Allen's Lock. Plain but hospitable village local serving Fullers and bar meals. Pool. Tel: 01869 232300.

Provisions obtainable from the canal shop at Oxfordshire Narrowboats.

TRAINS - local services along the Cherwell Valley. Useful staging-post for towpath walks. Details on 08457 484950.

THE Oxford Canal is arguably at its most charming and sublime between Heyford and Thrupp. It drifts through the delicious landscape of the Cherwell Valley like something out of the slow heart of a concerto. At Northbrook the canal bridge abuts a much older structure spanning the river. This carried a packhorse route across the Cherwell centuries before the canal was even thought of. A mile or two to the south lies the course of the Romans' Akeman Street which linked Cirencester and St Albans.

Immediately south of the course of the Roman road, the canal passes through a dark, emerald tunnel of overhanging trees, which retains an almost primeval quality that the legions must have been familiar, if not exactly at ease, with. In the heart of the wood lie the enigmatic ruins of an old cement works. The canal formed the only practical access to and from the site. Coal, sand and gypsum were brought in by boat and cement taken out, much of it travelling only as far as Enslow where it was transhipped to rail. The works closed in 1927, production being transferred to a new plant - itself now largely demolished - adjacent to Baker's Lock.

There used to be a pub called "The Three Pigeon's" by Bridge 213; hence the name of the adjoining lock. It must have been a welcome resort for the thirsty cement workers, but a long time has passed since the last pint was supped, though the building remains as a private residence, as does another of the Cherwell's former watermills. It's an idyllic quarter of an hour's walk from here - over sluice gates, millstreams and backwaters, and through cornfields - to the sleepy village of Tackley.

Just beneath the railway bridge at Enslow you can see old mooring rings set in the wall and the scars of unloading apparatus where the cement was transhipped from boats into railway wagons. Below Baker's Lock the canal merges with the river and sharp bends abound on the reach down to Shipton Weir Lock (Map 15).

Summary of Facilities

ROCK OF GIBRALTAR - adjacent Bridge 216. Tel: 01869 331686. Famous old canalside pub with a nice garden.
GARDINER ARMS - Tackley. Well-appointed, wisteria-clad pub offering an excellent choice of food. Tel: 01869 331266. Although it's a good 'country mile' away, you'll enjoy a visit to Tackley's village shop housed in the village hall and stocking a good range of locally produced farm foods.

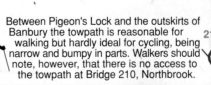

Northbrook

210
Northbrook Lock
5ft 0ins

209
Dashwood Lock
9ft 3ins

208

212

211

former quarry

70'

Akeman Street Roman Road

River Cherwell

Flights Mill

Pigeon's Lock
8ft 4ins

215

213 golf course

214

70'

Enslow Mill Wharf

SHARP BENDS!

River Cherwell

Enslow
Rock of Gibraltar

216

217
Baker's Lock
8ft 6ins

13

Tackley

Between Pigeon's Lock and the outskirts of Banbury the towpath is reasonable for walking but hardly ideal for cycling, being narrow and bumpy in parts. Walkers should note, however, that there is no access to the towpath at Bridge 210, Northbrook.

By-roads to A423, Woodstock etc

A4095 to Woodstock

AT Shipton Weir Lock canal and river part company, the Cherwell flowing south-eastwards past Islip to become that traditionally romantic stream of The Parks with its punts and its poets. Shipton Lock, like Aynho, is diamond shaped and not at all deep, but it can look as welcoming as a Cornish harbour in a gale when the navigable reach of the Cherwell is in spate. It is a remote spot, the old lock-keeper's cottage having been long ago demolished. Boaters from the local club at Thrupp use the backwater for picnics.

Lovers of ecclesiastical architecture will relish viewing the churches at Shipton and Hampton Gay. In the latter's graveyard a headstone commemorates one of the thirty-four passengers who died in the Christmas Eve railway tragedy of 1874, when a derailed train plunged into the icy waters of the neighbouring canal. Between bridges 220 and 221 the canal widens into a shadowy lagoon fringed by beds of water lilies and reeds. The canal builders are said to have diverted a millstream here and used

its course to form the canal. Onomatopoetically not unlike the sound of a boat engine, Thrupp consists of little more than a waterway maintenance yard housed in handsome buildings of thatch and honey-coloured stone, and a terrace of cottages fronting the canal as though it was a village street. This idyllic setting features as the location for a grisly murder in the Inspector Morse mystery *The Riddle of the Third Mile*. Colin Dexter also used the Oxford Canal in another Morse story, *The Wench is Dead*.

Thrupp might have become an important canal junction had 18th century proposals for a direct link between Hampton Gay and London ever got off the drawing board. The scheme was promoted in rivalry to the Grand Junction Canal and came about largely because of the poor state of the Thames at the time. In the event the Grand Junction received its Royal Assent first and the London & Western Canal, as it was to be known, languished, its subscribers receiving only sixpence back in the pound on their misplaced investment and optimism.

Thrupp	Kidlington
THE BOAT - Thrupp. A pub which features in many a canaller's 'Desert Island' choice of waterside inns. Sadly no longer Morrells beer but Greene King. Food, nice garden. Tel: 01865 374279. JOLLY BOATMAN - canalside Bridge 223. Main road pub, also popular with boaters. Bar and restaurant meals. Canalside seating area. Tel: 01865 373775.	Heavily suburbanised village chiefly useful for a quick ram-raid on reality. WISE ALDERMAN - canalside Bridge 224. Family pub with pleasant garden. Tel: 01865 372281. Co-op supermarket, shops and banks less than ten minutes walk from bridges 226 and 228. Spar shop close to Bridge 224.

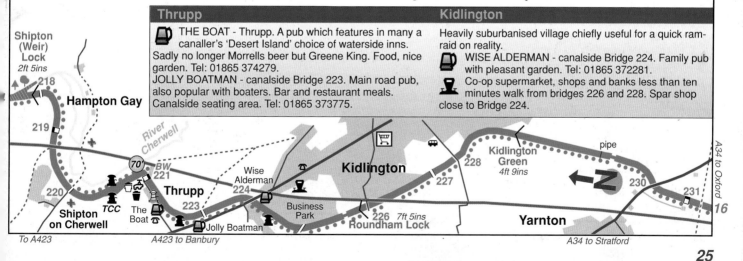

THE canal's approach to (and exit from) the university city of Oxford is low key. Not for it the ethereal landscapes of the Thames and Port Meadow or the Cherwell and The Parks. But rather - with the diffidence of a freshman arriving for Michaelmas Term - it slinks into Oxford by the tradesmens' entrance, making its way modestly past the foot of gardens belonging to the Victorian villas of North Oxford's erudite suburbs.

Coming south from Dukes Lock the countryside seems reluctant to take its cue and leave. Allotments and small holdings border the canal, as do a considerable number of residential boats. Gradually the suburbs begin to make their presence felt: the playing fields of St Edward's School; the imposing redbrick houses of well-heeled dons; and, inevitably, much new housing. Bridge 240 offers egress to Aristotle Lane, a useful general store, childrens' playground and The Anchor, and there may be some boaters who prefer to moor here away from the canal's crowded end.

Lucy's foundry is as old as the canal. Once they would cast you anything in iron you cared to mention; nowadays their order books are filled with car components. St Barnabus's church tower overlooks designated visitor moorings, and its lugubrious chime will invade your beauty-sleep. On the opposite bank, the terraced streets of Jericho (scene of another Morse murder enquiry) are fronted by the boatyard of College Cruisers.

An elegant cast iron bridge spans the entrance to LOUSE LOCK as the main line of the canal heads for its quiet oblivion, a couple

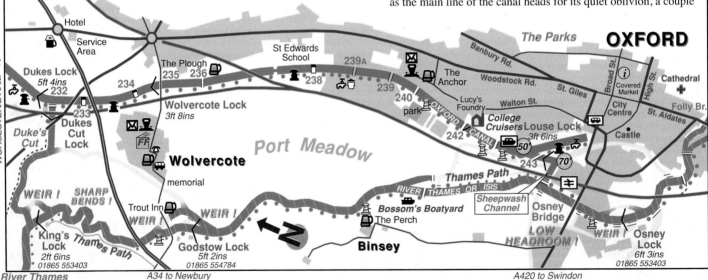

of hundred yards or so further on. Once upon a time the Oxford Canal terminated more grandiloquently in a broad basin of busy wharves overlooked by the castle keep. Business was brisk in coal brought down the cut from Warwickshire, and Temple Thurston came here in search of Eynsham Harry. But in 1937 the site was acquired by William Morris, alias Lord Nuffield, for the erection of a new college in his name. Since then the Oxford Canal has not so much terminated as petered out (although there are proposals to recreate the terminus) and, as the last few yards are largely occupied by residential boats, the visiting boater has no alternative but to moor somewhere back between bridges 239 and 243.

Turning needs to be considered as well: 50ft and under can turn in the winding hole by Bridge 243; anything longer than that and you'll have to go down through Louse Lock into one of the Thames backwaters to turn. Having got that far, it's difficult to resist the temptation to find your way out of Oxford via the Thames and Duke's Cut. To do this you'll need a Thames short stay licence. Suitably armed, you can proceed along the Sheepwash Channel (where sadly the yeoman of Oxfordshire no longer gather to dip their flocks) and pass beneath the railway; noticing, as you do, the rusty remains of a railway swingbridge which used to carry the line to the old London & North Western terminus on Rewley Road. Beyond the railway the channel emerges to join the Thames itself. You should turn right, upstream in the direction of Binsey and Godstow and Kings locks. A left turn would take you downstream to Reading as covered in *Pearson's Canal Companion to the Kennet & Avon and Middle Thames*.

The next reach is spellbinding. Soon the tree-lined banks open out to expose the full extent of Port Meadow where cattle and horses graze against a skyline of Oxford's dreaming spires. GODSTOW LOCK intervenes, but then it's worth mooring to the grassy bank upstream of Godstow's ancient stone bridge to explore the ruins of the nunnery where Henry II's mistress, Fair Rosamund, died. Or, considering the needs of the inner man, repairing to the famous "Trout Inn" overlooking the adjacent weir stream.

The Thames, also known as Isis hereabouts, meanders from Godstow to KING'S LOCK, and though you may have already fallen for its riverine ways, to regain the canal you must turn right above the lock and head back to the man made waterway. The main channel proceeds upstream to Lechlade as described in *Pearson's Canal & River Companion to the Severn & Avon and Upper Thames*. The Duke's Cut was actually the original link between the canal and the river, being opened in 1789. It was owned by the Duke of Marlborough, hence the name. Boats also used it to gain access to the now sadly defunct paper mill at Wolvercote, which relied on boatloads of Warwickshire coal until 1951. For many years the mill was owned by the Oxford University Press and specialised in the sort of wafer-thin paper used in the production of prayer books. All too soon, passing beneath the A40 and the railway, the little DUKE'S CUT LOCK returns you to the Oxford Canal.

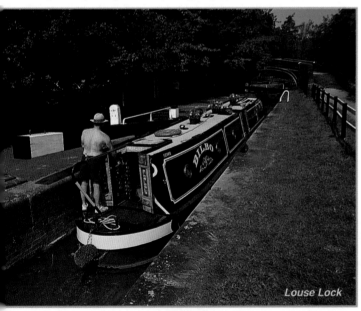

Louse Lock

Oxford (Map 16)

Oxford's pressures seem not so much 'Town & Gown' nowadays, as 'Town & Tourism'. Yet it can still remind you of an exclusive club, where the best the casual visitor can do is press their nose up against the lattice windowpane and peer enviously at the academically privileged world revealed within. Like Thomas Hardy's hero, we are all 'Obscure Judes', in awe of this world-renowned seat of learning. In Oxford - perhaps more than in any other English city - time stands quite literally still. Whole quadrangles and cloisters seem frozen into a medieval eternity where only the undergraduates ubiquitous bicycles break the chronological spell. From the perspective of the river boat, or the open-topped tourist bus, the sightseer can derive a vicarious wisdom. After all, you can now truthfully recall: "When I was at Oxford."

WATERMANS ARMS - riverside above Osney Lock. Tel: 01865 248832. Cosy local, bar food.

LAMB & FLAG - St Giles. Ancient inn associated with C.S. Lewis and Tolkien and, in recent years, one Endeavour Morse. Lunchtime food. Tel: 01865 515787.

THE NOSEBAG - St Michael's Street. Tel: 01865 721033. Long established wholefood cafe/restaurant.

FISHERS - St Clements. Close to Magdalen Bridge. Fish and seafood restaurant. Tel: 01865 243003.

THE PERCH - Thames-side, Binsey. Thatched riverside inn set back behind a mask of trees. Large garden, wide menu. Tel: 01865 240386.

THE ANCHOR - adjacent Bridge 240. Welcoming suburban pub serving food and Wadworths. Tel: 01865 510282.

FAR FROM THE MADDING CROWD - Friar's Entry. Tel: 01865 240900. CAMRA recommended free house.

QI - The Turl. Tel: 01865 261501. 'Quite Interesting' bookshop/cafe well worth seeking out by those of a literary and inquisitive bent.

BROWNS - Woodstock Road. Tel: 01865 511995. Well established brasserie converted from former Morris garage.

LE PETIT BLANC - Walton Street. Tel: 01865 510999. Raymond Blanc owned restaurant hidden away in the backstreets of Jericho.

Drawing on a wide range of custom and taste, Oxford's shops are inspired to an admirable eclecticism. The COVERED MARKET (off High Street) hosts the most wonderful cross-section of retailers and has an atmosphere almost unique in our experience. Perhaps only Bristol can compete in places linked by waterway terms.

(i) TOURIST INFORMATION - Broad Street. Tel: 01865 726871 www.visitoxford.org

CITY SIGHTSEEING - open top bus rides with running commentary. Regular departures from the railway station and city centre stops. Tel: 01865 790522.

THE OXFORD STORY - Broad Street. Ride through Oxford's rich history. Tel: 01865 728822.

MUSEUM OF OXFORD - St Aldates. Tel: 01865 815559.

ASHMOLEAN MUSEUM - Beaumont Street. Tel: 01865 278000. Britain's oldest public museum (not Mons) displaying European, Egyptian and Near Eastern antiquities.

CARFAX TOWER - Carfax. 99 steps to heaven for a bird's eye view of the city of dreaming spires.

PUNT HIRE - Oxford's most traditional means of seduction can be hired from boat houses at Folly Bridge on the Thames and Magdalen Bridge on the Cherwell.

COLLEGES - over thirty colleges make up Oxford University. Many of them are world famous such as Balliol and Merton which are both of 13th century origin; Magdalen (pronounced 'Maudlin') which dates from 1458; and Christ Church founded in 1525 by Cardinal Wolsey. The general public may look around most of them in the afternoons.

OPEN SPACES - much of Oxford's charm rests in the proliferation of green spaces, the city's lungs. These include: The Parks, Christ Church Meadow and Port Meadow. A stroll - or a picnic - on any of them comes as a refreshing experience after the hurly burly of the main thoroughfares and helps put Oxford in the context of its riverside setting.

TRAINS - services along the Thames Valley to/from Reading and London and connections to/from the midlands and the north. Tel: 08457 484950.

BUSES - contact the Oxford Bus Company on 01865 785400.

Wolvercote (Map 16)

Residential suburb situated between the canal and the Thames. Useful post office stores less than 5 minutes walk to west of Bridge 235 plus Chinese take-away (Tel: 01865 310439) and frequent buses to/from Oxford city centre. In Upper Wolvercote, to the east of the canal, THE PLOUGH (Tel: 01865 556969) can be accessed from Bridge 236.

The Grand Union Canal

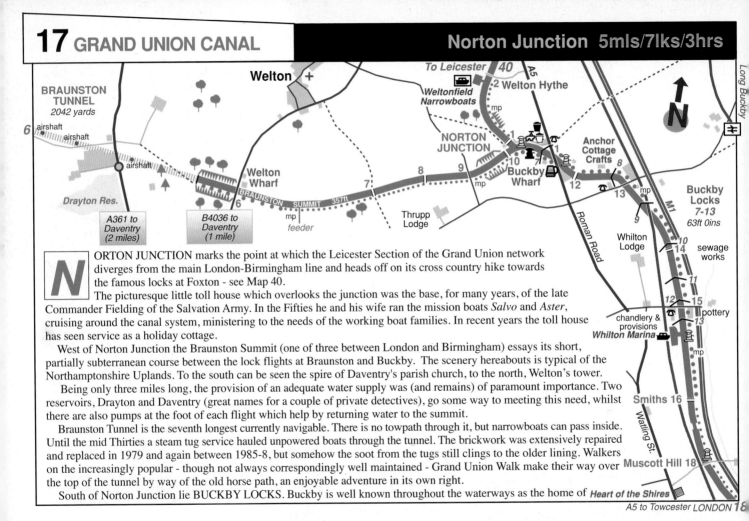

Welton

To Leicester 40

Weltonfield Narrowboats

2 Welton Hythe

BRAUNSTON TUNNEL
2042 yards

6 airshaft
airshaft
airshaft

NORTON JUNCTION

Anchor Cottage Crafts 8

Drayton Res.

Welton Wharf

1
10 7
1
Buckby Wharf

8 9
7 mp
12

BRAUNSTON SUMMIT 357ft
6 feeder
mp

Thrupp Lodge

13 9

Buckby Locks 7-13
63ft 0ins

A361 to Daventry (2 miles)

B4036 to Daventry (1 mile)

Whilton Lodge

10
14 sewage works

11

chandlery & provisions
Whilton Marina

12 15
13 pottery

mp

Smiths 16

Watling St.

Muscott Hill 18

A5 to Towcester LONDON 18

NORTON JUNCTION marks the point at which the Leicester Section of the Grand Union network diverges from the main London-Birmingham line and heads off on its cross country hike towards the famous locks at Foxton - see Map 40.

The picturesque little toll house which overlooks the junction was the base, for many years, of the late Commander Fielding of the Salvation Army. In the Fifties he and his wife ran the mission boats *Salvo* and *Aster*, cruising around the canal system, ministering to the needs of the working boat families. In recent years the toll house has seen service as a holiday cottage.

West of Norton Junction the Braunston Summit (one of three between London and Birmingham) essays its short, partially subterranean course between the lock flights at Braunston and Buckby. The scenery hereabouts is typical of the Northamptonshire Uplands. To the south can be seen the spire of Daventry's parish church, to the north, Welton's tower.

Being only three miles long, the provision of an adequate water supply was (and remains) of paramount importance. Two reservoirs, Drayton and Daventry (great names for a couple of private detectives), go some way to meeting this need, whilst there are also pumps at the foot of each flight which help by returning water to the summit.

Braunston Tunnel is the seventh longest currently navigable. There is no towpath through it, but narrowboats can pass inside. Until the mid Thirties a steam tug service hauled unpowered boats through the tunnel. The brickwork was extensively repaired and replaced in 1979 and again between 1985-8, but somehow the soot from the tugs still clings to the older lining. Walkers on the increasingly popular - though not always correspondingly well maintained - Grand Union Walk make their way over the top of the tunnel by way of the old horse path, an enjoyable adventure in its own right.

South of Norton Junction lie BUCKBY LOCKS. Buckby is well known throughout the waterways as the home of *Heart of the Shires*

Norton Junction

the 'Buckby Can'. These metal water carriers, adorned with 'roses & castles', were an essential piece of the boat families' inventory, because their boats were not equipped with water tanks and running water from the tap. Watling Street crosses the canal at Buckby Wharf and here the towpath changes sides. A pedestrian tunnel lengthens the odds of negotiating the A5 in one piece.

For a couple of miles the canal is in close proximity to the M1 motorway and correspondingly loses much of its inherent peace and quiet. The ghosts in this landscape must be severely disturbed, but ghosts there must be, for the Roman settlement of Bannaventa stood adjacent to what is now Whilton Marina, and the medieval village of Muscott lay adjacent to Bridge 18.

Summary of Facilities *(Map 17)*

There's only one pub remotely near the canal on Map 43 and that's the well-known NEW INN (Tel: 01327 844747) by Buckby Top Lock which offers Frog Island ales from Northampton along with home-cooked food, eponymous Rose & Castle cans for sale, skittles to play and a resident ghost called 'Matilda'.
Stroll up from Bridge 18 to the HEART OF THE SHIRES shopping village (open daily, ex Mons), a group of specialist shops (including a tea room and a deli) housed in what was a Victorian 'model' farm. Those all important holiday souvenirs may be purchased at ANCHOR COTTAGE CRAFTS (between bridges 12 and 13), WHILTON LOCKS POTTERY (Bridge 15), or at the WHILTON CHANDLERY (beside Whilton Marina), where provisions are also on sale.

TRAINS - useful staging post for towpath walkers at Long Buckby station 1 mile east of Bridge 13. Central Trains. Tel: 08457 484950.

WHEN Napoleon was busy acquiring as much of Europe as he could early in the 19th century, the Government got out a map of England and looked for somewhere safe to hide King George III. Their eye fell upon the tiny Northamptonshire village of Weedon Bec which, not entirely coincidentally, had just been linked to London with the completion of William Jessop's Grand Junction Canal. Here they built barracks and a Royal Pavilion. A canal arm led off the main line, entering the barracks through a portcullis. It was obviously intended that Weedon would be defended to the last. Happily, Bonaparte met his match elsewhere, and the King never needed to use his splendid pavilion. But the barracks remained in use for many years and, on occasions, troops were carried by canal boat from here to troublespots and ports of embarkation.

A 15 mile pound separates the lock flights at Buckby and Stoke Bruerne. To maintain this horizontality, the canal accommodates the undulations of the countryside: wrapping itself around the sinuous valley of the upper Nene, and crossing the river by way of a high embankment at Weedon.

As the canal curves round Nether Heyford there are views in the distance of Heygates flour mill on the Nene at Bugbrooke.

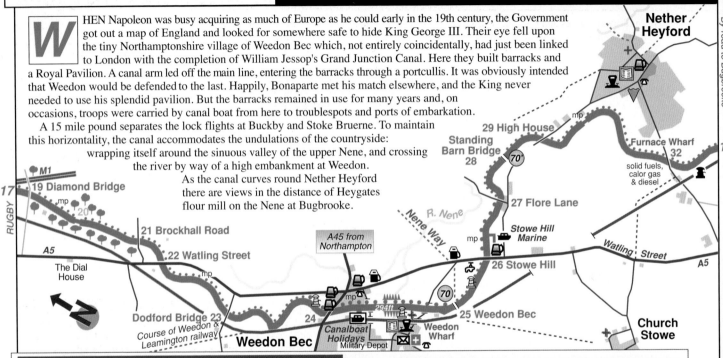

Weedon

Down from Bridge 24 you'll come upon a cornucopia of antique shops, but the quieter core of Weedon lies to the west, well away from the A5, where the vast barracks may be seen, though not officially explored.

Pubs proliferate - take your pick from the HEART OF ENGLAND (Tel: 01327 340335) by Bridge 24, the PLUME OF FEATHERS (Tel: 01327 340978) in 'real' Weedon west of the canal or THE GLOBE (Tel: 01327 340336) and CROSSROADS HOTEL (Tel: 01327 340354) which overlook the junction of the A5 and A45. MING'S COURT (Tel: 01327 349818) is a Chinese restaurant and take-away also adjacent to Bridge 24. THE NARROWBOAT (Tel: 01327 340536), beside Bridge 26, is a Charles Wells pub offering food and motel style accommodation.

The village shops are located west of the canal and best reached from the offside moorings on the embankment near the church. They include a general stores, post office, and a pharmacy. Buses link Weedon with Daventry and Northampton - Tel: 0870 608 2 608.

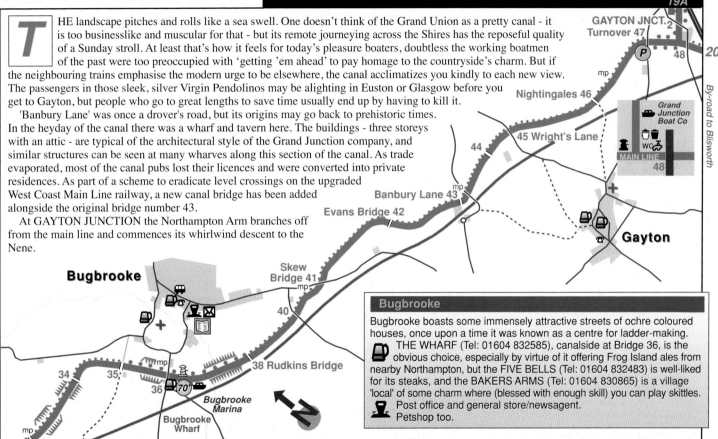

T HE landscape pitches and rolls like a sea swell. One doesn't think of the Grand Union as a pretty canal - it is too businesslike and muscular for that - but its remote journeying across the Shires has the reposeful quality of a Sunday stroll. At least that's how it feels for today's pleasure boaters, doubtless the working boatmen of the past were too preoccupied with 'getting 'em ahead' to pay homage to the countryside's charm. But if the neighbouring trains emphasise the modern urge to be elsewhere, the canal acclimatizes you kindly to each new view. The passengers in those sleek, silver Virgin Pendolinos may be alighting in Euston or Glasgow before you get to Gayton, but people who go to great lengths to save time usually end up by having to kill it.

'Banbury Lane' was once a drover's road, but its origins may go back to prehistoric times. In the heyday of the canal there was a wharf and tavern here. The buildings - three storeys with an attic - are typical of the architectural style of the Grand Junction company, and similar structures can be seen at many wharves along this section of the canal. As trade evaporated, most of the canal pubs lost their licences and were converted into private residences. As part of a scheme to eradicate level crossings on the upgraded West Coast Main Line railway, a new canal bridge has been added alongside the original bridge number 43.

At GAYTON JUNCTION the Northampton Arm branches off from the main line and commences its whirlwind descent to the Nene.

Bugbrooke

Bugbrooke boasts some immensely attractive streets of ochre coloured houses, once upon a time it was known as a centre for ladder-making. THE WHARF (Tel: 01604 832585), canalside at Bridge 36, is the obvious choice, especially by virtue of it offering Frog Island ales from nearby Northampton, but the FIVE BELLS (Tel: 01604 832483) is well-liked for its steaks, and the BAKERS ARMS (Tel: 01604 830865) is a village 'local' of some charm where (blessed with enough skill) you can play skittles. Post office and general store/newsagent. Petshop too.

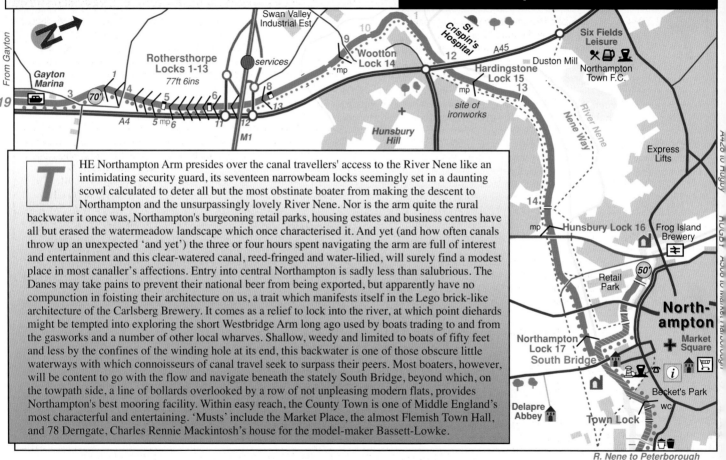

From Gayton

19

Gayton Marina

70'

A4

Rothersthorpe Locks 1-13
77ft 6ins

services

Swan Valley Industrial Est

Wootton Lock 14

mp

Hunsbury Hill

M1

St Crispin's Hospital

A45

12

Hardingstone Lock 15

13

mp

site of ironworks

Duston Mill

Six Fields Leisure

Northampton Town F.C.

River Nene

Nene Way

Express Lifts

14

mp

Hunsbury Lock 16

Frog Island Brewery

50'

Retail Park

North-ampton

Northampton Lock 17 South Bridge

Market Square

Delapre Abbey

Town Lock

Becket's Park

wc

T HE Northampton Arm presides over the canal travellers' access to the River Nene like an intimidating security guard, its seventeen narrowbeam locks seemingly set in a daunting scowl calculated to deter all but the most obstinate boater from making the descent to Northampton and the unsurpassingly lovely River Nene. Nor is the arm quite the rural backwater it once was, Northampton's burgeoning retail parks, housing estates and business centres have all but erased the watermeadow landscape which once characterised it. And yet (and how often canals throw up an unexpected 'and yet') the three or four hours spent navigating the arm are full of interest and entertainment and this clear-watered canal, reed-fringed and water-lilied, will surely find a modest place in most canaller's affections. Entry into central Northampton is sadly less than salubrious. The Danes may take pains to prevent their national beer from being exported, but apparently have no compunction in foisting their architecture on us, a trait which manifests itself in the Lego brick-like architecture of the Carlsberg Brewery. It comes as a relief to lock into the river, at which point diehards might be tempted into exploring the short Westbridge Arm long ago used by boats trading to and from the gasworks and a number of other local wharves. Shallow, weedy and limited to boats of fifty feet and less by the confines of the winding hole at its end, this backwater is one of those obscure little waterways with which connoisseurs of canal travel seek to surpass their peers. Most boaters, however, will be content to go with the flow and navigate beneath the stately South Bridge, beyond which, on the towpath side, a line of bollards overlooked by a row of not unpleasing modern flats, provides Northampton's best mooring facility. Within easy reach, the County Town is one of Middle England's most characterful and entertaining. 'Musts' include the Market Place, the almost Flemish Town Hall, and 78 Derngate, Charles Rennie Mackintosh's house for the model-maker Bassett-Lowke.

R. Nene to Peterborough

BLISWORTH and Stoke Bruerne are contrasting canalside communities separated by the third* longest presently navigable tunnel in Britain. It takes around half an hour to pass through; time to reflect upon the tunnel's eventful history. By the time the rest of the Grand Junction Canal had opened between London and Braunston in 1800, Blisworth still wasn't finished, despite having been under construction for seven years. A temporary tramway over the top of the hill was built in its place - traces of which are still visible - and goods were laboriously shipped from boat to wagon and back again. Finally the tunnel was opened on 25th March 1805.

Blisworth Tunnel's dimensions permitted narrowboats to pass inside, but no towpath was provided. At the outset boats were poled through, rather in the manner of Oxford punts, but this practice was apparently abandoned in favour of the more traditional art of 'legging', though with, not surprisingly, a considerable number of fatalities. The canal company provided registered leggers who wore brass arm bands proclaiming their role. Later, as traffic increased, a steam tug service was provided, and although this was withdrawn as long ago as 1936, there is still a reek and an aroma of soot and steam to be savoured within the tunnel's confines. Amongst various bicentenary celebrations in 2005, was the legging of the Fellows Morton & Clayton boat *Sunny Valley* through the tunnel while a boat horse was led by suitably costumed enthusiasts over the top.

In the late 1970s, in common with many other impressive canal structures, Blisworth Tunnel was feeling its age, and suffering from a backlog of indifferent maintenance. Its lining deteriorated to such an extent that it became necessary to close the tunnel for four years, effectively severing the canals of the Midlands from those of the South-East. Four million pounds were spent on re-lining the bore, and the tunnel re-opened, amidst much ceremony, and not a little relief amongst the boating fraternity, in August 1984.

The Grand Union skirts Blisworth, passing beneath the A43 and the West Coast Main Line in the process. This area was once riddled with iron stone quarries linked by tramway to loading stages along the canal bank, much of the stone being carried the comparatively short distance by boat to Hunsbury Hill Furnaces on the Northampton Arm (Map 19A). Blisworth railway station was the junction for the Stratford & Midland Junction Railway discussed in the text accompanying Map 9 as well as the line from Blisworth to Peterborough which used to accompany much of the course of the River Nene.

Blisworth Mill, a handsome brick building once used as a depot by the Grand Union Canal Carrying Company, but now, perhaps inevitably, converted into housing, overlooks Bridge 51. Blisworth Tunnel's northern portal is built from blue brick. Half an hour after entering the tunnel you can compare this with the redbrick of the southern portal.

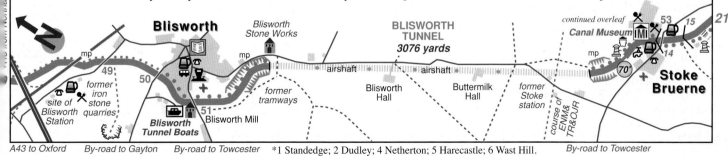

Blisworth

Blisworth Stone Works

BLISWORTH TUNNEL 3076 yards

airshaft — airshaft

continued overleaf — Canal Museum

53 — 15 — 21

Stoke Bruerne

mp — 49 — 50 — site of Blisworth Station — former iron stone quarries — 51 — Blisworth Mill — Blisworth Tunnel Boats — former tramways — Blisworth Hall — Buttermilk Hall — former Stoke station — course of ENM& TR&OJR — 70° — 14 — mp

A43 to Oxford — By-road to Gayton — By-road to Towcester — *1 Standedge; 2 Dudley; 4 Netherton; 5 Harecastle; 6 Wast Hill. — By-road to Towcester

continued from previous page

Given the gradients, walkers might be hard pushed to keep pace with the boats beneath them. Moreover they are likely to be beguiled by side shows: tramway earthworks, airshafts, the imposing premises of Blisworth Stone Works, and the haunted trackbed of the grandiloquently titled Easton Neston Mineral & Towcester, Roade & Olney Junction Railway. The astonishingly capacious station building at Stoke Bruerne is still occupied domestically, well over a century after its passenger services ceased, a mere four months following its opening in 1891; thus meagre proved the custom here and at the next station to the east, Salcey Forest. But trains still pounded through Stoke for another sixty years or so, amongst them Race Specials bound for Towcester, and Midland Railway banana trains enduring a circuitous journey from Avonmouth Docks to Fyffes depot at Somers Town in London.

Where Blisworth dreams, Stoke Bruerne bristles; both with boaters and tourists, the latter attracted here primarily by the village's famous Canal Museum. Steerers should handle their craft with consideration and courtesy, keeping a special eye open for the trip boats which ply between the winding hole and the top lock. As the cutting recedes, the canal narrows through the site of Rectory Bridge, then widens as it reaches the wharf and associated buildings which, taken as a whole, make Stoke Bruerne such an attractive canal location.

A three-storey, stone built mill dominates the wharf. Once it ground corn with machinery driven by steam, now it houses the celebrated museum, first opened to the inquisitive public as long ago as 1963. A basin for boats delivering coal to the mill lay behind where the tall poplar trees now stand, and all trace has vanished of the roving bridge which carried the towpath over the entrance to this dock. A row of stone cottages, originally provided for millworkers, but later used by canal employees, separates the mill from a brick house of Georgian style. The Georgian house was for many years a shop catering for the needs of boating families. But in the twilight years of commercial carrying it was the home of Stoke's favourite daughter, Sister Mary Ward, a lady of high ideals and humility, who took it upon herself to look after the boat people in sickness and in health until her retirement in 1962.

As trade expanded on the Grand Junction Canal, it became necessary to duplicate the locks. Here at Stoke it is interesting to discover that the

Bridge 47 near Gayton

top lock in use today is the duplicate chamber, the original being on the west side of the canal and used nowadays to accommodate a boat-weighing machine from the Glamorganshire Canal and a BCN 'station boat', both being amongst the museum's outdoor exhibits; similarly the narrowboat *Sculptor* which is usually moored outside the mill unless attending a boat rally elsewhere. Buildings on the west bank of the canal include the wharfinger's office and house, now occupied by canal author and water transport campaigner, David Blagrove. David's book, *Bread Upon the Waters*, paints a vivid description of life on the Grand Union Canal towards the end of commercial carrying in the 1960s. Another worthwhile read featuring Stoke Bruerne is John Thorpe's *Windlass in my Belt*. Brian Collings of the Guild of Waterway Artists, painter of our 'signwritten' covers for many years, and a consummate painter in oils of transport subjects also lives in Stoke Bruerne.

Traditionally no mooring was allowed in the Stoke flight, but recently rings have been provided in the comparatively lengthy pound between locks 15 and 16 where once an arm provided access to a brickworks which has been transformed into a nature reserve. To the west lies Stoke Park and a pair of privately owned pavilions which once flanked a much larger property designed by Inigo Jones in the first half of the 17th Century.

Blisworth *(Map 20)*

Church and chapel dominate the view from the canal, and there are some fine looking stone buildings, reminders of the village's significance as a centre of quarrying.

ROYAL OAK - up from Bridge 51. CAMRA recommended village 'local' offering bar and restaurant food. Hook Norton and guest beers. Pool, darts and skittles. Tel: 01604 848372.

General store, and newsagent (dealing in local heritage items) on High Street.

BUSES - to/from Northampton, Towcester and Milton Keynes. Tel: 0870 608 2 608.

Stoke Bruerne *(Map 20)*

Against the odds, Stoke Bruerne transcends its popularity. In high season it attracts the sort of ice cream crowds which many a theme park would be proud of. Yet it contrives to retain its integrity, remaining a tight-knit community with a mildly obsessive interest in the welfare and activity of its canal. For this is a canal village without equal, and the Grand Union runs through it like a High Street, so that for once boaters see front doors and windows rather than back.

THE BOAT INN - canalside above top lock. Expanded 'local' popular with visitors and villagers alike which has been run by the same family for four generations. Restaurant with view over canal to mill and museum. Bistro, breakfasts, provisions. Frog Island, Adnams, Marston's etc. Tel: 01604 862428.

THE NAVIGATION - canalside Bridge 53. Family pub with canal-themed interior. Tel: 01604 864988.

BRUERNE'S LOCK - canalside restaurant, sophisticated menu. Tel: 01604 863654.

OLD CHAPEL - rear of museum. Attractive tearooms and restaurant. Tel: 01604 863284.

Stoke Bruerne

CANAL MUSEUM - Tel: 01604 862229. Housed in a corn mill which closed before the Great War, the museum opened in 1963, having developed from the personal collection of local lock-keeper, Jack James. Indoor exhibits include canal folk costumes, an operational model of Anderton Lift, and many other fascinating, evocative and topical displays. The museum shop houses probably the best range of canal literature anywhere in the country. If you haven't a complete set of up to date *Canal Companions* then here's an opportunity to fill the gaps. Out of doors a preserved narrowboat is usually on view together with other bits and pieces of canal history too bulky to find a home inside. Significantly, the museum seems in no way to have been eclipsed by the establishment of the prestigious National Waterways Museum at Gloucester and we can wholeheartedly recommend it to boaters and other visitors alike. Open daily 10am to 5pm in Summer. Closed all day Monday in Winter and shuts at 4pm. Admission charge.

NORTHAMPTONSHIRE is a county more travelled through than visited. Lines of communication stretch across its hedged fields like strings across the frets on the neck of a guitar. Perhaps that's why these roads and railways, and this canal, appear aloof from the landscape. "Sorry, can't stop," they seem to be saying: "We're just passing through."

The canal traveller spends two hours negotiating the six mile pound between Stoke Bruerne and Cosgrove: a lonely landscape characterised by ridge & furrow pasturelands. Besides a diverting succession of wide spill-weirs, the only major landmarks are the manor house and church on the brow of the hill at Grafton, the wharf and mooring lagoon at Yardley (where you are warned to beware 'elderly ducks'), and the lofty, flying-buttressed spire of Hanslope church to the east.

Few outside the county of Northamptonshire will claim to know the course of the River Tove, but by the time it joins the Great Ouse at Cosgrove it is a significant watercourse. It rises on the uplands east of Banbury, not far from Sulgrave Manor. At the foot of Stoke locks one arm of the river - used for private moorings - flows into the canal, whilst the other passes beneath the man made waterway. The Tove forms the boundary with Buckinghamshire, a county which stretches surprisingly far north, even for those who like to feel they have a firm grasp on topography.

Stoke Locks form another step in the Grand Union's roller-coaster ride between London and Birmingham: the old Grand Junction Canal had summits at Tring and Braunston; when the route was amalgamated with the Warwick & Birmingham Canal in 1929 a third summit was added at Olton near Solihull. A pump house, dated 1939, returns water from the foot of the flight to the top, but another water saving economy, the use of side ponds, is no longer in use.

Considering its status as a long distance canal walk between London and Birmingham, the towpath between Stoke Bruerne and Cosgrove is ill-maintained. Encroaching vegetation makes it uncomfortable for walkers and downright impossible for cyclists.

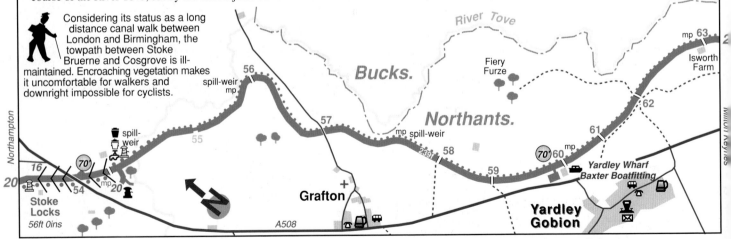

THAT old adage about the River Trent being the boundary between North and South conveniently ignores the existence of the Midlands. But here, between Cosgrove and Wolverton, the Great Ouse creates a very real sense of demarcation, separating the murky Midlands from the salubrious South, though, for a while at least, the roles seem reversed, as the canal traverses the urban sprawl of Milton Keynes to the south and the unspoilt countryside of the Tove Valley, sprinkled with stone-built villages, to the north.

High embankments prepare the canal, but not necessarily the canal traveller, for the leap across the Ouse. One moment you are on a seemingly everyday length of waterway, the next you are apparently in mid air without the benefit of a parachute. Thirty five feet below the Ouse flows unconcernedly, and all that prevents you from joining it is the narrow lip of the aqueduct's iron trough. But, unlike Pontcysyllte, these high jinks are over in a flash, and boaters really wanting to appreciate the structure should moor nearby, return on foot, and crouch through the cattle creep beneath the embankment to get a better view, albeit a view compromised by abundant growths of willow and reed which detract somewhat from the aqueduct's impact. As for the river itself, can this sluggish watercourse, turgidly flowing over jettisoned supermarket trolleys, really be the same Great Ouse which pours with such velocity out into The Wash at King's Lynn?

Just above COSGROVE LOCK a short arm used as private moorings indicates the route of the former Old Stratford & Buckingham branch, a much mourned rural canal which paralleled the course of the River Ouse between here and Buckingham. It opened in 1801,

Continued overleaf

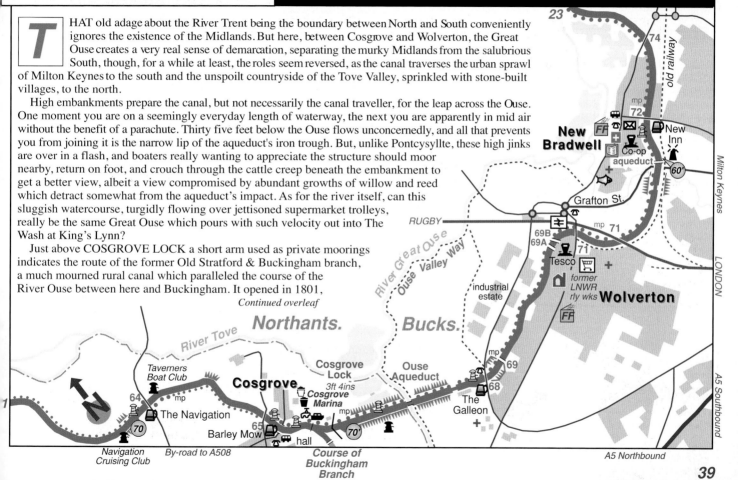

39

continued from overleaf

measured ten miles and had two locks. But it was never much of a commercial success, being used primarily for the carriage of agricultural produce, particularly hay and straw used as fodder by London cab horses. In the event it was devoid of traffic by the 1930s and officially abandoned in 1954. Attempts to have it restored were baulked when the A5 by-pass was built across its bed near Old Stratford. Perhaps the most interesting facet of its operation was the establishment of a boatbuilding yard, away from the canal itself, at Stony Stratford specialising in the construction of small sea-going vessels which had to be hauled by traction engine along the Watling Street and launched into the canal for transfer to London.

WOLVERTON, once famous for its railway works, and continued home of the Royal Train, imposes a sense of dreariness on the canal. A grave sadness lurks implicitly behind all those broken-windowed, red-brick workshops where generations of crimson lake coloured carriages were proudly built and expertly maintained. Buddleia, convolvulus and meadowsweet thrive now in the absence of lost activity and the canal escapes in a broad arc around the village of NEW BRADWELL. In working boat days the boat women would hobble down the hill in their voluminous skirts to shop, catching up with their unstopping boats at the other end of the embankment. They would not recognise the huge new aqueduct carrying the canal over Grafton Street; moreover, it seems unlikely that its designers, Pell Frischman, will join Telford and Rennie in the pantheon of bridge builders. Up on the hillside the sails of a restored windmill peep over the treetops, whilst down in the valley of the Ouse flooded-out sandpits have created attractive expanses of water.

Cosgrove (Map 22)

A quiet village away from the main road with some attractive stone buildings. On the off-side a fine row of poplar trees frames the parkland of the hall. An unusual pedestrian tunnel (once used by boat horses to reach the pub stables) passes beneath the canal, whilst, for reasons never satisfactorily explained, Bridge 65 is unusually ornate. Sand was worked commercially down by the confluence of the Tove and Ouse. A narrow gauge railway linked the sand pits with the canal wharf and some of the rails remain in situ by the old canal junction.

THE NAVIGATION - canalside Bridge 64. A deservedly popular stone pub, good choice of food together with a range of real ales from the Greene King portfolio. Tel: 01908 543156.

BARLEY MOW - offside south of Bridge 65. Customer moorings. Food, skittles & garden. Tel: 01908 562957.

Groceries obtainble from the caravan park adjacent to Cosgrove Lock.

BUSES to/from Northampton and Milton Keynes - Tel: 0870 608 2 608.

Wolverton (Map 22)

Wolverton is something of an interloper, a manufacturing town seemingly cast adrift from its Midlands moorings and washed aground in rural Buckinghamshire. Plenty of facilities for passing boaters: corner pubs, ethnic restaurants and fish & chips. THE GALLEON (Tel: 01908 313176) is a well known pub with a canalside garden adjacent to Bridge 68 where the canal widens and there are good moorings. TESCO (24 hour) and NETTO supermarkets easily reached from Bridge 71; Lloyds & Barclays banks. Frequent local services from canalside station. Tel: 08457 484950. Taxis - Tel: 01908 313030.

New Bradwell (Map22)

A community of terraced streets built as homes for the employees of Wolverton railway works. Useful shops within a stone's throw of Bridge 72 and a nice pub, THE NEW INN (Tel: 01908 312094) offering Adnams, Wells and guest real ales as well as bar and restaurant meals and a pleasant garden. There are Chinese and Indian takeaways, too, but best of all is NAPOLI the wonderful fish & chip shop on Newport Road, owned by second generation Italian, Luciano Pilla - Tel: 01908 313193.

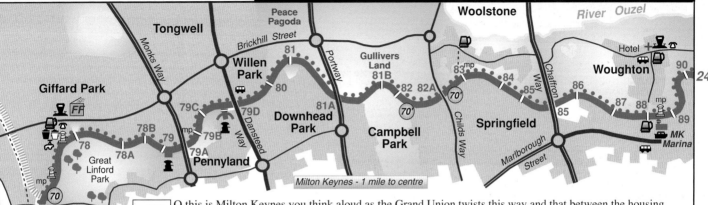

SO this is Milton Keynes you think aloud as the Grand Union twists this way and that between the housing developments. And how you respond is as much a matter of taste and outlook as the car you drive and the coffee you drink. The variety of architectural styles is as diverse as it is eclectic. One welcomes the good honest use of brick and timber, the refusal to be hidebound and categorised; the informality, the heterogeneity, the vernacular splashes of weatherboarding and pantiles; the canal's role as a linear park. But what comes as a surprise is the sheer un-Englishness of it all: communal drives, patios and lawns seem at odds with native Anglo-Saxon reserve, as though Milton Keynes was the blueprint for a new generation of gregarious Britons. But, inevitably, there are disappointments. One would have welcomed more integration of houses and water; more examples of the admirable Pennyland Basin, where arms have been allowed to penetrate in and around individual dwellings, so that those inhabitants with boats can 'park' them in aquatic driveways.

Amidst all these Brave New World developments, it is easy to forget that the canal predates the city by a century and a half. Old maps show the canal traversing a rolling landscape of scattered hamlets, and the working boatmen of the past would surely be astonished at the transformation. The only canalside settlements of any note along this section were at Great Linford and Woughton on the Green. The former was notable as the point from which a branch canal led to Newport Pagnell. It had been opened in 1817 but was closed by 1846, much of its course being taken over by a branch railway, itself now converted into a pleasant public footpath. The newly proposed canal between Milton Keynes and Bedford - targeted to open in 2010 at a cost of £150 million - will happily, therefore, bring back a junction to the Grand Union in the neighbourhood, though initial surveys suggest that this could be in the vicinity of Bridge 82A.

Great Linford (Map 23)

Magically idyllic manorial village sympathetically encapsulated within the new city's development zone. Moor up and stroll along its neatly gravelled paths; listen to the birdsong; watch the pond life; admire the church, manor and almshouses. PROUD PERCH - canalside Bridge 76 - is a refurbished 'all-day' pub with a nice waterside garden offering bar and restaurant food. Tel: 01908 398461.

Giffard Park (Map 23)

A new housing development of chief interest to canal users for its facilities. The GIFFARD PARK (Tel: 01908 210025) is a Brewers Fayre pub. Across the road you'll find a post office (with cash machine), convenience store, Chinese takeaway (Tel: 01908 615205) and off licence. Buses leave at frequent intervals for the city centre.

Milton Keynes (Map 23)

MK leapt off the drawing board in the early 1970s, identified as the location for a new city designed, initially, to house 150,000 re-settled Londoners. Twenty-two thousand acres - absorbing the settlements of Bletchley, Wolverton, Stony Stratford and New Bradwell - were commandeered from the North Buckinghamshire countryside and laid down in a grid-pattern of roads linking designated areas of housing, commercial, industrial and leisure zones. When we originally encountered Milton Keynes - during compilation of the first edition of this guide back in the 1980s - it seemed far ahead of its time and quite unlike any other British city. Now, however, there is a familiar ring to it, as if consciously, or unconsciously, MK's Brave New World has become a blueprint for us all.

PEARTREE BRIDGE INN - canalside Bridge 88. Toby Inn. Tel: 01908 691515.

YE OLDE SWAN - Woughton. East of Bridge 88. 'Village' pub. Tel: 01908 679489.

PARKSIDE HOTEL - Woughton. Accessible from Bridge 88. Restaurant and bars open to non-residents. Tel: 01908 661919.

The main shopping area lies between Midsummer and Silbury Boulevards about one and a half miles west of the canal: 'half a mile of covered shopping'!

TOURIST INFORMATION CENTRE - Midsummer Boulevard. Tel: 01908 558300.

GULLIVERS LAND - Bridge 81B. Children's theme park. Tel: 01908 200010.

PEACE PAGODA - 5 minutes walk from Bridge 81. A thousand specially planted cherry and cedar trees enshrine the memory of victims of all war, whilst the pagoda itself, erected in 1980 by the nuns and monks of Nipponaan Myohoji - stands in the specific hope that the earth will be spared from nuclear annihilation.

BLETCHLEY PARK - Bletchley (accessible by bus from MK or train from Fenny Stratford (Map 24). AKA 'Station X', the now celebrated home of codebreaking in WWII. Tel: 01908 640404.

BUSES - an excellent network of 'Street Shuttles' provides easy access to/from the city centre. Tel: 0870 608 2 608.

TRAINS - InterCity and local services from station in Central MK. Tel: 08457 484950.

TAXIS - Tel: 01908 555555.

Stoke Hammond

FENNY STRATFORD Lock marks the commencement of the Grand Union's climb out of the valley of the Ouse up towards the Chilterns and the summit at Tring. But, with a rise of a meagre foot, its contribution to the ascent is not impressive. In fact, it was not planned in the original survey, being built as a supposedly temporary measure to alleviate excess water pressures experienced on the long pound between here and Cosgrove. Tradition has it that southbound working boats in a hurry used to burst their way through whichever gates happened to be shut at the time, a habit the authorities would doubtless respond to with court summonses today. In any case, the lock comes as welcome exercise after the three or four hours spent glued to the tiller if you have come straight down from Cosgrove.

'Finney' marks the southern extent of Milton Keynes' sprawl. Travelling southwards it is, in many ways, reassuring to be back in the familiar world of semi-detached suburbs. Fenny Wharf was a busy spot: coal was brought to the gas works and flour and sugar carried from London Docks to Valentine's mill. As the canal emerges from its urban environment there are pleasant views across the River Ouzel and Watling Street towards the elevated heathlands of Woburn and Aspley. Northwards from Fenny Stratford the Grand Union is bordered briefly by factories before skirting the old village of Simpson on an embankment. A small aqueduct, invisible from the waterline, accommodates a footpath. There are glimpses to the east of Walton Hall, headquarters of the Open University.

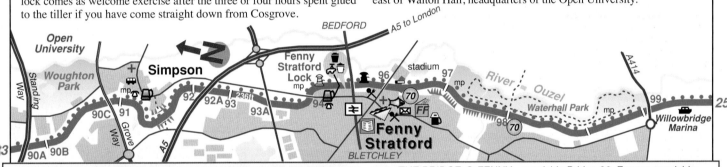

Simpson

Another of Milton Keynes' antecedent villages. Buses to the city centre and a public phone. THE PLOUGH (Tel: 01908 670015) is a Charles Wells pub with a garden backing on to the canal serving bar and restaurant meals.

Fenny Stratford

A former coaching village on the old Watling Street, Fenny Stratford seems somewhat out on a limb and forgotten now, though there are good reasons for boaters to break their journey here, not least good restaurants and the provision of water, Elsan and rubbish disposal facilities.

THE BRIDGE @ FENNY - canalside Bridge 96. Former canalside pub refurbished as a stylish restaurant. Tel: 01908 379584.
RED LION - lockside local. NAPOLI'S - Aylesbury Street. Italian fish & chips from the same family as at New Bradwell; eat in or take out. Tel: 01908 372457. COLOSSEO - Aylesbury Street. Italian coffee and sandwich bar. Tel: 01908 645588. DINAJPUR - Aylesbury St. Les Routiers recommended Indian. Tel: 01908 376234.

'Finney' is bereft of food shops, and probably MK is to blame for that, but there is a splendidly traditional ironmongers called POLLARDS.
TRAINS - Fenny Stratford is on Silverlink's Bletchley to Bedford route. Tel: 08457 484950. TAXIS - Tel: 01908 646565.

T HE Grand Union has probably appeared more often in canal literature than any other waterway. Classics, fictional and factual, like *The Water Gipsies, Hold on a Minute, Maiden's Trip,* and *Bread Upon the Waters,* successfully capture its atmosphere as a working waterway, but don't really prepare you for its beauty as it unravels through the Ouzel Valley, past the sandy, bracken covered hills of Linslade and over the border from Bucks to Beds. The Ouzel seems to shift some of its riverine quality upon the canal; as in all good friendships, there is a degree of exchange in character. Between bridges 109 and 111 the "Cross Bucks Way" offers towpath walkers a pretty detour above the canal past the isolated church and manor house at Old Linslade.

The Ouzel rises on Dunstable Downs and flows northwards to join the Great Ouse at Newport Pagnell. It used to be a river of many watermills, some of which survive very prettily as private dwellings. SOULBURY LOCKS - known to working boatmen as the 'Stoke Hammond Three' (which sounds more like an organ-based jazz combo) - they are overlooked by a popular pub. A picnic site and car park add to their gongoozling

appeal, and if any of your crew suffer from stage fright this is not the best place for them to freeze whilst operating the locks.

The three mile pound between Soulbury and Leighton locks is captivating. Beyond the watermeadows of the Ouzel mixed woodland clothes a ridge of heathland.

Summary of Facilities

Two well known canalside pubs tempt you to pause along this length of canal. At Soulbury Locks the eponymous THREE LOCKS (Tel: 01525 272393) does a roaring trade with motorists fascinated by the activity of the locks. A wide range of meals are served and the pub is open all day in summer. Of equal popularity, THE GLOBE (Tel: 01525 373338) by Bridge 111 is a much older building, attractively weatherboarded outside and beamed within. Various real ales, bar and restaurant meals and a fine canalside patio.

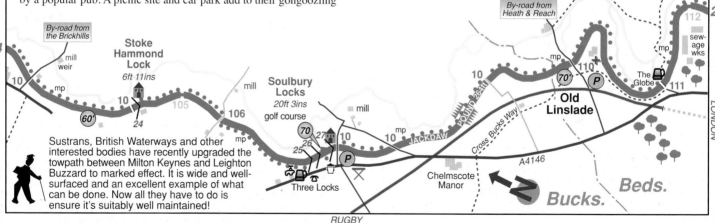

Sustrans, British Waterways and other interested bodies have recently upgraded the towpath between Milton Keynes and Leighton Buzzard to marked effect. It is wide and well-surfaced and an excellent example of what can be done. Now all they have to do is ensure it's suitably well maintained!

*I*NTERRUPTED briefly - but not overwhelmed - by the shared urban environments of Linslade and Leighton Buzzard, the Grand Union Canal continues its predominantly rural progress, crossing the boundary between the counties of Bedford and Buckingham. Solitary locks come along at regular intervals, each with its own atmosphere and ambience. Leighton Lock is overlooked by a substantial, whitewashed lock-keeper's house; by Grove Lock there is a stone milepost advertising the distance to the Thames; and adjacent to Church Lock what was once the smallest chapel in Buckinghamshire has been converted into a private residence.

In the early years of the Grand Junction water shortages were experienced and, to go some way to alleviate the problem, a sequence of narrowbeam chambers were duplicated alongside the original wide locks.

These allowed single boats to use less water and also enabled the canal to cope better with its growing traffic. Remains of these locks are apparent at several locations and explain the provision of extra arches on a number of bridges. A series of pumping engines was also introduced to return water to the summit. Most of the characteristic engine houses remain. By and large they are gaunt and ghostly structures now, redolent of a time when the canal was in business to make a profit for its shareholders; though one or two have been adapted for new use. Working boatmen called them the 'Northern Engines', and naturally there were regular deliveries of coal by boat to stoke the boilers. Another local cargo was sand and there is plenty of evidence of former wharves, some still with track embedded in the towpath where narrow gauge railways ran to connect such loading points with the sand pits themselves. One of these lines has transformed itself into a delightful passenger-carrying line - Tel: 01525 373888.

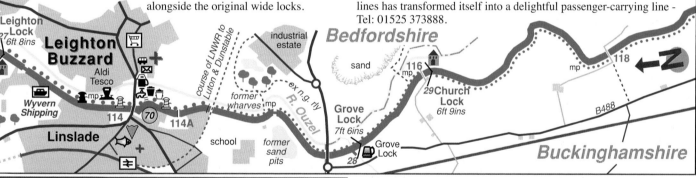

Leighton Buzzard

An unexpectedly delightful town with a refreshing period feel; especially on Tuesdays and Saturdays when the handsome High Street throbs with the activity of a street market. A wealth of solid, provincial architecture spans the centuries - a perfect antidote to the high-tech of Milton Keynes, elevating Leighton into probably the most interesting town on the whole of the old Grand Junction.

GROVE LOCK - canalside Lock 28. New restaurant/pub dispensing Fullers excellent beers.Tel: 01525 380940. *Plenty of pubs, fish & chips and takeaways in Leighton itself, not so much choice in Linslade.*

Some distinctive local shops in the town centre, notably H.G.STRATTON an award- winning butcher/baker on Market Square - Tel: 01525 372183. Canalside TESCO, town centre WAITROSE.

TRAINS - frequent Silver Link services along the Northampton-Milton Keynes-Berkhamsted corridor. Tel: 08457 484950.

SAND gives way to clay, and clay to chalk, as the canal begins to take seriously the need to climb up to The Chilterns. Locks occur more frequently, and there is little point in those responsible for working them reboarding the boat in the intervening pounds. In any case it's fun to tramp along the towpath for a change, gazing eastwards to the furzy escarpment of the Dunstable Downs where, on a clear day, you can make out the chalk lion of Whipsnade and watch gliders making the most of upwardly mobile thermals above the rounded rampart of Ivinghoe Beacon. A mile and a half south-east of Bridge 123 is Ivinghoe and its National Trust windmill.

A sense of remoteness settles over the countryside. The boat people knew this stretch of canal as "The Fields", a typically simple yet eloquent description. The isolation is underlined when you recall that the Great Train Robbery took place on the lonely section of line north of Cheddington station in 1963.

The Grand Junction was a canal obsessed with time. Everything was date-stamped: lock chambers, bridges, tie bars, mooring rings, paddle gear. You are tempted to indulge in a sort of Victorian parlour game in which you must attach an important event to each date you come across.

Boating is brisk by Cooks Wharf where the Dunstable & District Boat Club have extensive moorings. Round the corner, tucked in between the road and railway bridges, is Grebe Canal Cruises' busy boatyard which boasts its own cafe.

Cheddington

This straggling commuter village, noted for fruit growing, can be reached by road from Horton and Cooks wharves, or by lane and path from Ivinghoe Locks.

OLD SWAN - quaint, thatched pub south of village centre best reached from Bridge 126. Tel: 01296 668226.

DUKE OF WELLINGTON - Cooks Wharf (reached to south of Bridge 126). Bar meals daily. Tel: 01296 661402.

General store and post office in village centre with cash machine.

TRAINS - isolated station (from which there are views of Mentmore once the country seat of the Rothschilds) served by trains between Milton Keynes and London Euston, forming a useful staging post between Leighton Buzzard and Tring for the benefit of towpath walkers. Tel: 08457 484950.

TAXIS - Cheddington Taxis. Tel: 01296 661666.

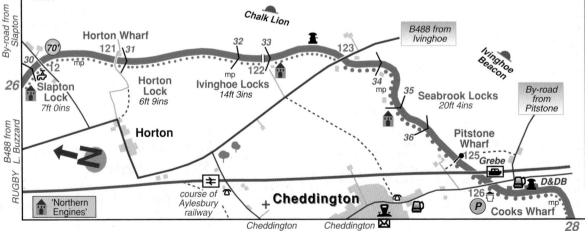

created by the setting of the reservoirs. From MARSWORTH JUNCTION the Aylesbury Arm commences its lovely journey down to the county town of Buckinghamshire. Its course is fully described in the text accompanying Map 28A.

BULBOURNE JUNCTION lies immediately above the top chamber of the Marsworth flight. It forms an attractive canalscape, a covered drydock and a junction house providing particularly graceful features. The Wendover Arm brings a welcome supply of water into the main line. The six mile branch was built primarily with this role in mind, though a flour mill and the famous boatbuilding yard of Bushell Bros. brought extra activity. Seepage caused abandonment of the central section of the arm in 1904, but little by little it is rewardingly being brought back to life, most recently by virtue of the provision of a new winding hole to the west of Bridge 3. Here, in idyllic surroundings, are 48 hour visitor moorings with swallows for company during the summer months, though you are responsible for bringing your own Amazons. It is a detour well worth making. Freshly pumped

continued overleaf

MARSWORTH - or, in the patois of the working boatman, "Maffers" - is a key location on the old Grand Junction's route between London and Braunston. Here the canal drops from its Tring Summit and, in doing so, crosses the boundary between Hertfordshire and Buckinghamshire. Seven wide locks used up their fair share of water and, as traffic grew, a series of reservoirs were constructed to keep the canal in water. The Upper and Lower courses of the prehistoric Icknield Way (now known as the B488 and B489 respectively) cross the canal at either extremity of the flight. The road connected East Anglia with Salisbury Plain. A delightful account of its course was written by Edward Thomas - perhaps better known as a poet than a topographical writer - and published in 1916, a year before he was killed at the Battle of Arras. His text, however, pays scant attention to the canal, other than to remark on a certain 'foreign' character

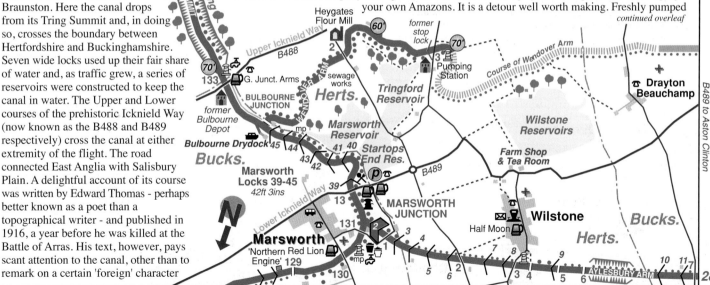

up from the reservoirs, the water is decidedly clear; clear enough to spy giant pike basking in the prolific weed. Progress by boat is necessarily slow, but soon the first overbridge appears and, immediately beyond it, a large and flourishing flour mill. It was here, where Heygates park their lorries now, that Bushells had their boatyard. Tringford pumping station stands adjacent to a former stop lock, west of which the arm reaches its current terminus, though the towpath is comfortably walkable all the way to Wendover. Formed in 1989, the Wendover Arm Trust aims to restore navigation back to Wendover. An information box containing leaflets about both the Arm and the Trust's activities is located at BULBOURNE JUNCTION; it may be opened with a standard BW 'Watermate' key.

Just south of the junction stand the elegant Bulbourne workshops where lock gate manufacture took place until recently. However British Waterways have now abandoned the site and it is now partially occupied by a firm specialising in ornamental ironwork who have a gallery open to the public. Beyond the depot the canal passes beneath the Upper Icknield Way and enters TRING CUTTING. Stretching for one and a half miles, and reaching a maximum depth of thirty feet, the cutting is said to have taken the best part of five years to dig. With equipment no more sophisticated than pick-axes and wheel-barrows, this is not a surprising statistic. But the labour of two centuries ago seems nebulous now. Nature long ago reclaimed the gash in her side, soothed it with vegetation, and created a chasm of narcotic splendour.

Aylesbury (Map 28A)

In spite of its status as the county town of Buckinghamshire, Aylesbury is a comparatively small place. It became an administrative centre when Buckingham was partially destroyed by fire in 1725. One's first impressions are tainted by a surfeit of glass, concrete and traffic. But somehow the old heart of the town survives, grouped about the market place with its cobbles, statues, clocktower and handsome municipal buildings. Deeper into the town, along attractive lanes and alleyways, and you come upon the substantial parish church of St Mary's - the highest and probably the most peaceful point in Aylesbury.

THE SHIP - cosy little street corner pub backing on to the basin, serving bar food, Fullers and Greene King ales. Tel: 01296 421888. KING'S HEAD - Market Sq. Tel: 01296 381501. Remarkable 15th century inn with courtyard. Now operated (even more remarkably) by the National Trust. Also features a bookshop! Lunches Mon-Sat and beers from the excellent local brewer Chiltern.
CARLO'S - Temple Street. Tel: 01296 423021. Lively Portuguese restaurant.
The town centre is a five minute walk from the canal basin. Two indoor precincts are occupied by most household names. Tesco by Lock 16, Morrisons beside the railway station.
TOURIST INFORMATION CENTRE - Bourbon Street. Tel: 01296 330559.
BUCKINGHAMSHIRE COUNTY MUSEUM - Church Street. Admission free. Everything you always wanted to know about Bucks and a gallery devoted to Roald Dahl which children will love. Tel: 01296 331441.
BUSES - services throughout the area. Tel: 0870 608 2 608.
TRAINS - services to/from London Marylebone. Train buffs will enjoy the branchline ride to Princes Risborough, especially peak hour workings operated by a 1960 vintage single unit railcar. Tel: 08457 484950.

Marsworth (Map 28)

A quiet, unassuming village on the border of Bucks and Herts, dominated by a nice flint-towered church. Three pubs and a tea room but *no* shops!
RED LION - adjacent Bridge 130. Classic village pub long favoured by canal travellers. Buckinghamshire brewed Vale beers feature; comfortable sofas, comforting food ordered at the kitchen door. Tel: 01296 668366. WHITE LION (Tel: 01442 822325) by Bridge 132. ANGLERS RETREAT (Tel: 01442 822250), down the road from Bridge 132. Or try BLUEBELL'S TEAROOMS (and craft shop) by Lock 39 - Tel: 01442 891708.
BUSES - regular Aylesbury-Dunstable service. Tel: 0870 608 2 608.

Bulbourne (Map 28)

No shops, but the GRAND JUNCTION ARMS (Tel: 01442 890677) by Bridge 133 is a popular pub with a large garden. Good choice of food including breakfasts from 8.30am. Beers include Adnams.

Wilstone (Map 28)

Small village alongside the Aylesbury Arm. Little pub called the HALF MOON - all beams and gleaming brass - Tel: 01442 826410, as well as a well-stocked village store, and farm shop with tea room on B489.

28A GUC AYLESBURY ARM

*I*N common with the Northampton Arm, the Aylesbury Arm has the dubious distinction of featuring a considerable number of locks in a comparatively short distance. But the Aylesbury Arm's attraction lies not so much in the steepness of the gradient as in the tranquillity of its setting. Once you have negotiated the staircase lock at Marsworth (Map 28) you are ravished by the immediate and utter intimacy of the arm, which proceeds to spill down into the Vale like an apple-cart rumbling along a country lane. In fields bordering the canal, pigs frolic in the mud and hens scrat for tasty morsels on a dung heap. For a couple of miles the arm passes into Hertfordshire, but the landscape remains aloof, the inherent peace of the canal being broken only by the hooting of car horns as they approach each hump-backed bridge.

At this point you will probably be impatient for facts, even though, as Sir John Squire once ruefully pointed out, they are only flies in the amber. But the bare essentials are that the canal was promoted late in the 18th century as a through route across the Vale of Aylesbury to the Thames at Abingdon, from whence connection could be made via the Wilts & Berks and Kennet & Avon canals to Bath and Bristol. What a mouth-watering canal odyssey that would have made possible. However, only the arm to Aylesbury materialised and, following its opening in 1815, it settled down to a century and a half of trade, notably to and from Nestles now mothballed factory near the terminus of the arm and through the carrying activities of the well known boat company Harvey-Taylor.

Although the Aylesbury Arm is essentially a rural canal there is much to see and discuss. As you proceed across the border into Herts there are views to the north of Mentmore, designed by Paxton for one of the Rothchilds. Soon the flint tower of Marsworth church is left astern and, as the gradient eases, the locks come less closely spaced. Lock 9 is sweetly called 'Gudgeon Stream'.

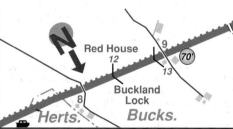

Red House Lock is named after an isolated inn of the same name which stood alongside it, but which was converted into a private residence in the mid Sixties. Beyond here the channel narrows perceptibly and the reeds seem to whisper like conspirators as you pass. Presently the outskirts of Aylesbury make their presence felt and, though the towpath quality improves, industry then takes over; notably Nestles whose plant once provided so much trade for the canal. Two demure lines of terraced houses, linked by a footbridge, herald the L-shaped terminal basin with its friendly community of residential boats. You may even be welcomed by a member of the local canal society and pointed politely to a suitable mooring in the shadow of the Inland Revenue office block which dominates the basin. Relax, overnight moorings are tax deductible.

Details of Aylesbury and its facilities appear on page 48.

Aylesbury
Aylesbury Basin
Town Centre
A41 Akeman Street
Tesco
industrial estate
Aylesbury Locks
18
17
16
15
16A
16
15
14
Broughton Lock
14
13
1 12
10
Red House
12
70'
13
9
Buckland Lock
8
Herts. Bucks.
Bates Boatyard

N

TRING'S three mile summit section extends from Bulbourne to Cowroast. As the canal emerges from Tring Cutting there used to be views eastwards above the beechwoods to the urn-topped column which stands on Aldbury Common, about a mile and a half east of Tring railway station. The past tense is deliberate, because the trees now seem to have grown too high for the top of the monument to be seen from the canal. So you will need to make a pilgrimage on foot to pay homage to this monument, erected in 1832 in memory of the doyen of canal promoters, Francis Egerton, the third Duke of Bridgewater. The neighbouring estate of Ashridge House was one of the 'Canal Duke's' properties, albeit one that he allowed to fall into ruin. Inside the column a staircase climbs to a viewing balcony two hundred feet above the ground. Owned now by the National Trust, it is open to the public on summer weekends - Tel: 01442 851227.

In contrast to the graceful splendour of the Duke's monument and its sylvan setting, the opposite bank of the canal is occupied by business units developed from a former 'Buffer Depot', a semi-secret Government establishment used for the storage of supplies held pending a national emergency. This one abuts a well-piled wharf, suggesting that the Civil Service had more faith in the Grand Union's capacity for commercial trade than British Waterways.

COWROAST is a popular boating centre, a lagoon providing moorings for private craft off the main line. The lock here is picturesque and well cared for. Look out for the pump house, the cast-iron span of Bridge 137 (protected by lozenge-shaped weight restriction notices) and the former Control Office responsible for correlating

boat movements up and down the Grand Union in carrying days. South of Cowroast the 'Grand Junction' commences its journey down to the Thames at Brentford. A steady procession of locks takes the canal along the valley of the River Bulbourne. Tennis courts, recreation grounds and a non-league football stadium herald the approach to BERKHAMSTED, a civilised town which clearly takes a pride in the appearance of its canal and, by the same token, creates a favourable impression with canal travellers be they on foot or afloat. Graffiti and vandalism are conspicuously absent as the canal moves agreeably along its corridor between the railway and the A4251. A series of attractive plaques interpret local history, from which you derive many gems, such as that in 1852 a man from Clun in Shropshire set up a works in Berkhamsted to manufacture the world's first commercially produced sheep-dip from arsenic and sulphur. A canalside totem pole (genuine and imported from

Map labels

castle

142
55
A4251
141 Berkhamsted Locks 53-55 *16ft 10ins*
Berkhamsted Town F.C. 53
High Street
("Gas Two") 52
51
mp
Waitrose
Berkhamsted

14
("Bushes") 50
Sports Centre
Tunnel
Northchurch Common
49 139
Northchurch Locks 49-52 *27ft 0ins*
Northchurch
R. Bulbourne
mp
138
Dudswell
48
47
Dudswell Locks 47 & 48 *13ft 4ins*

RUGBY
Bridgewater Monument
By-road from Aldbury
Cowroast Lock *6ft 0ins*
46
Cowroast Marina
mp
137
13
mp
70'
391ft
28 TRING SUMMIT
Cowroast
A4251 to Aylesbury

Canada by the owner of a timber yard which stood on the site before it was redeveloped for housing) creates extra interest as the canal negotiates Berko's trio of locks, passing close to the impressive motte & bailey remains of Berkhamsted Castle. Geoffrey Chaucer was Clerk of Works here and Thomas a'Becket the castle's Constable at one time. In more recent times the town's most famous citizen has been Graham Greene who was born on Chesham Road (just off the High Street) in 1904, his father being a housemaster - and subsequently headmaster - of Berkhamsted School, a substantial campus encountered by canallers walking to the High Street from bridges 141 or 142. The canal is mentioned in a number of Greene's works, and he autobiographically recalls 'that odd gritty smell blowing up from the coal barges' and fictionally 'the smell of wet leaves and canal water'.

When the Grand Junction arrived in Berkhamsted at the end of the 18th century it kick-started a raft of new industries and Castle Wharf gained the sobriquet 'Port of Berkhamsted'. Timber yards, a grain mill, a coal wharf, a gas works (hence the pair of locks nicknamed 'Gas Two'), and a boatbuilding yard all brought trade to the canal, and naturally a bevy of pubs to slake the boatmen's famous thirst.

Berkhamsted

19th century Berkhamsted was a centre of straw-plaiting for the hatmakers of Dunstable and Luton. Now it's a vibrant residential town with a handsome traffic-calmed High Street, a most pleasant place for sauntering, window-shopping or just 'promenading' on warm summer evenings. Many fine buildings combine to create a favourable impression: the 16th century Monks House (now a French restaurant); the Town Hall (now a French restaurant) and St Peter's Church (which hasn't become a French restaurant - yet!).

CRYSTAL PALACE - Bridge 141. Tel: 01442 862998. Canalside near the railway station. Design inspired by Paxton, hence the name.
THE BOAT - Bridge 142. Tel: 01442 877152. A modernised Fullers pub.
RISING SUN - Tel: 01442 864913. An unspoilt boatman's pub nicknamed 'The Riser' overlooking Lock 55.
OLD MILL - offside between Lock 55 and Bridge 143 (Map 30). Chef & Brewer restaurant. Tel: 01442 879590. Limited customer moorings.
ASK - 247 High Street. Tel: 01442 878287. Stylish modern Italian restaurant.
CAPE FISH - High Street. Tel: 01442 879988. Modern seafood restaurant.
CAFE ROUGE - 296 High Street. Tel: 01442 878141. Well known French chain.

Berkhamsted's little shops are full of character and include an award winning butchers called EASTWOODS by Bridge 142 (Tel: 01442 865012) who picked up The Independent's 'Organic Shop of the Year' prize in 2005. In contrast WAITROSE have a supermarket beside the canal.

TRAINS - frequent Silverlink trains between London Euston, Milton Keynes and Northampton, calling at Tring, Cheddington and Leighton Buzzard specifically, perhaps, for the benefit of towpath walkers. Tel: 08457 484950.

Cowroast

Nothing to do with bovine barbecues, but a corruption of 'cow rest', a throwback to cattle droving days. The COW ROAST inn (Tel: 01442 822287) predates the canal and serves bar and restaurant meals. A walk to Aldbury (a mile north-east of Bridge 136) will reward you with two nice country pubs: THE GREYHOUND and THE VALIANT TROOPER.

TRIBUTARIES of the Thames (and tributaries of the tributaries) usher the Grand Union down towards London's spreading tentacles. Initially it's the River Bulbourne that shapes the journey, from time to time indulging in congress with the canal, and then, below Hemel Hempstead, the Gade (which flows off the Dunstable Downs) takes up the running. Chalk streams both, in earlier times they were valued for their watercress, and evidence of former beds can here and there be seen. Perhaps the sewage works at Bourne End put an end to such innocent activities, or perhaps watercress is force-grown more economically elsewhere for our voracious supermarkets now.

The Bulbourne also drove its fair share of mills. A corn mill remains intact between locks 59 and 60, albeit much extended and converted into an hotel. Swing-bridge 147 is electrically operated nowadays and you will need a BW key to access the control panel.

Joseph Buck, the lock-keeper at Winkwell, went to a watery grave in the canal on Christmas Day 1898, probably as a result of too much festive spirit. The original graceful cast ironwork of Robert Stephenson's railway bridge between locks 61 and 62 has been insensitively coated in concrete.

The canal crosses the River Bulbourne and runs alongside Boxmoor Common to Two Waters and the river's confluence with the Gade. A pleasant cricket ground borders Boxmoor Lock, below which there are good moorings. Commercial traffic survived from London Docks to Hemel Hempstead until 1981, when Roses ceased handling casks of imported lime juice at the wharf below Bridge 151 now occupied by B&Q.

Hemel Hempstead

Do the denizens of Dacorum act with due decorum? Responses are subjective, suffice it to say that the architecture of Hemel Hempstead's post war new town contrasts tellingly with the original old town to the north, pinpointed by the spire of St Mary's church.

THREE HORSESHOES - canalside Winkwell Swing-bridge 147. Tel: 01442 862585. Pre-dates the canal by a little matter of three centuries! FISHERY INN - canalside Bridge 149. Famous boaters pub featured in Tim Wilkinson's seminal *Hold On A Minute*. KS - Balti restaurant alongside Bridge 151. Tel: 01442 239993.

The new town's shopping precinct lies about eight minutes walk north of Bridge 151. Handily practical, therefore, but not a patch on the old town's High Street beyond, an altogether more enjoyable shopping experience.

TOURIST INFORMATION - Marlowes Shopping Centre. Tel: 01442 234222. www.dacorum.gov.uk

Severn tug, 'Nashes Two'

HISTORICALLY, the neighbourhood of Apsley had strong associations with the manufacture of paper, an activity begun by the Fourdrinier brothers in the vicinity at the end of the 18th century. Apsley and Nash mills further developed under the stewardship of John Dickinson & Co. and the canal played a significant role in the inward carriage of coal and outward despatch of finished products. An express boat service known as the Paper Mill Dashers operated between Apsley and Dickinson's warehouses in Paddington, 8 hours being taken to cover 35 miles and 23 locks! Nash Mill remains in use, but the once vast Apsley Mill has largely been redeveloped as housing. Warwickshire coal continued to come down to the paper mills by narrowboat until the 1960s. The relationship between the mill owners and the canal company was not necessarily harmonious in the early days of the Grand Junction. Problems with water supplies to the mills necessitated construction of a canal deviation in 1819. A new course to the south of the original was adopted, incorporating a length of the River Gade, whilst four relatively deep and water-wasteful locks were replaced by five shallower ones, hence 69A at Kings Langley.

Another well known source of traffic for the canal was the Ovaltine works adjacent to Bridge 158. Sadly the factory, opened in 1913, closed in 2002 when production of the famous bedtime drink was transferred to Switzerland; all a far cry from the soporific beverage's 1930s heyday and the childrens 'League of Ovaltinies'. The company operated their own fleet of narrowboats apparelled in an eye-catching advertising livery, and even had a dairy and an egg farm. The works has been incoporated in a new housing scheme.

Apsley

Increasingly popular stopover for boaters lured by British Waterways marina facilities, Sainsbury's supermarket and a growing list of canalside establishments at which to eat and drink. Try THE WATERSIDE (Tel: 01442 232402) for breakfasts, lunches, dinners, and coffee and pastries between.

Kings Langley

12th century birthplace of Nicholas Breakspear, the only Englishman to become the Pope, Kings Langley is one of those rare villages which looks better by road than by boat. Suburban infills are responsible for this, but the High Street, strung out along the old London to Aylesbury road, is worth seeking out.

Here you'll find a wide choice of eating and drinking places, notably, LA CASETTA, an award-winning Italian. Tel: 01923 263823. There is also a good choice of shops including a butcher, two chemists, post office, SPAR, off licence, launderette, delightfully old-fashioned stationers, and even a model railway shop; though oddly no bank!

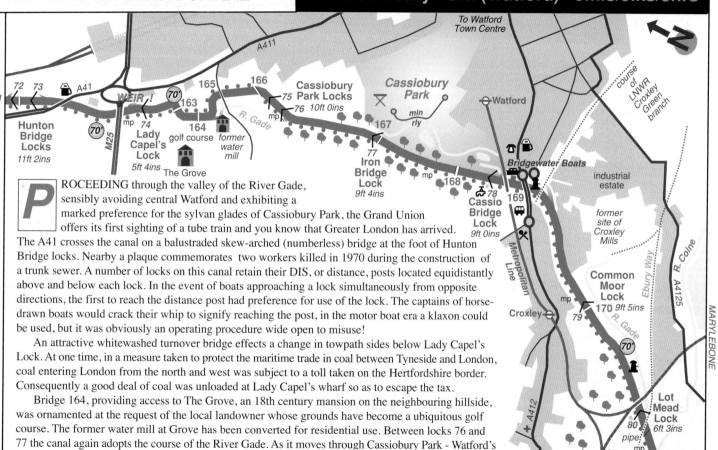

To Watford Town Centre

A411

72 73 A41

WEIR ! 70'

165

166

Cassiobury Park Locks

75

76 10ft 0ins

Cassiobury Park

min rly

Watford

course of LNWR Croxley Green branch

70'

M25

mp 74

Lady Capel's Lock

5ft 4ins The Grove

163

164

golf course

former water mill

R. Gade

167

77

Iron Bridge Lock

9ft 4ins

mp 168

78

Cassio Bridge Lock

9ft 0ins

169

Bridgewater Boats

industrial estate

former site of Croxley Mills

R. Colne

A4125

Hunton Bridge Locks

11ft 2ins

PROCEEDING through the valley of the River Gade, sensibly avoiding central Watford and exhibiting a marked preference for the sylvan glades of Cassiobury Park, the Grand Union offers its first sighting of a tube train and you know that Greater London has arrived. The A41 crosses the canal on a balustraded skew-arched (numberless) bridge at the foot of Hunton Bridge locks. Nearby a plaque commemorates two workers killed in 1970 during the construction of a trunk sewer. A number of locks on this canal retain their DIS, or distance, posts located equidistantly above and below each lock. In the event of boats approaching a lock simultaneously from opposite directions, the first to reach the distance post had preference for use of the lock. The captains of horse-drawn boats would crack their whip to signify reaching the post, in the motor boat era a klaxon could be used, but it was obviously an operating procedure wide open to misuse!

An attractive whitewashed turnover bridge effects a change in towpath sides below Lady Capel's Lock. At one time, in a measure taken to protect the maritime trade in coal between Tyneside and London, coal entering London from the north and west was subject to a toll taken on the Hertfordshire border. Consequently a good deal of coal was unloaded at Lady Capel's wharf so as to escape the tax.

Bridge 164, providing access to The Grove, an 18th century mansion on the neighbouring hillside, was ornamented at the request of the local landowner whose grounds have become a ubiquitous golf course. The former water mill at Grove has been converted for residential use. Between locks 76 and 77 the canal again adopts the course of the River Gade. As it moves through Cassiobury Park - Watford's

Metropolitan Line

Croxley

A412

Ebury Way

R. Gade

Common Moor Lock

mp 170 9ft 5ins

79

70'

Lot Mead Lock

6ft 3ins

80 pipe

mp

MARYLEBONE

green lung - the canal becomes a popular haunt for strolls and picnics. A marina occupies the site of Cassio Bridge wharf which served Watford. Those London Underground trains rattle across the high bridge of the Metropolitan Railway. Scarcely less imposing, but now abandoned, the old London & North Western Railway branch to Croxley Green spans the canal south of Bridge 169.

Croxley Paper Mills were the last to receive regular deliveries of coal by narrowboat around 1970. Widebeam boats brought cargoes of esparto grass up from Brentford. The site is now covered by new housing.

Squat tube trains rub shoulders with their altogether taller Chiltern Trains cousins on the railway bridge above Lot Mead Lock. At its tail, the River Gade briefly joins the canal for the last occasion before it becomes the River Colne, which rises to the south of St Albans, having accommodated, en route, the River Ver. Some charming, not to say eccentric residential craft are moored below Lot Mead Lock. The abandoned Watford & Rickmansworth railway - electrified as early as 1927 - has become a popular traffic-free path for walkers, cyclists and horse-riders known as the Ebury Way after Lord Ebury of Moor Park who promoted the railway. Its passenger services acquired the delightful sobriquet of 'watercress trains' as they were often used to carry the locally grown commodity to Watford market. Electrified or not, the line closed to passenger services in 1952. It is, however, not unknown for itinerant guide book writers to walk along its trackbed imitating the sounds of vanished electric trains.

Rickmansworth (Map 33)

A typical small 'Home Counties' town, self-sufficient despite its obvious proximity to London. The churchyard of St Mary the Virgin provides an attractive route into the town.

ZAZA - Church Street. Tel: 01923 772287. Mediterranean restaurant.

MAURIZIO'S - Church Street. Tel: 01923 775701. Italian.

THAI GEORGE - Church Street. Tel: 01923 776779.

COY CARP - canalside Bridge 177. Tel: 01895 821471. All day family pub with wide choice of food.

EDWINNS - Tel: 020 728 66752. Classy restaurant on outskirts of Harefield which can be reached along the lane to the east of Black Jack's Lock. Pricey but well worth it according to correspondents Toby and Ruth Bryant of our esteemed publishers, CWS.

HORSE & BARGE - adjacent Wide Water Lock. Tel: 01895 834080. Family pub with large garden.

Large TESCO with customer moorings on off side between bridges 173 & 174. Nice High Street of traditional shops in town centre 5 minutes walk from Batchworth Lock.

BATCHWORTH LOCK CANAL CENTRE - Tel: 01923 778382 www.rwt.org.uk

Moorings on the Chess

YET another river, the Chess, adds the weight of its waters - admittedly not that considerable - to the canal as Rickmansworth is approached. An unusual arrangement sees the provision of a side lock which once provided access to wharves upstream, primarily the brewery of Samuel Salter and Rickmansworth's gas works. This bosky backwater is now used for private moorings. Batchworth Lock was a busy point when the canal was at its zenith. Stabling was provided, part of which has been adapted as a canal interpretation centre and the base for a trip-boat operation southwards to Stocker's Lock.

A plaque on the wall of the substantial Tesco supermarket between bridges 173 and 174 recalls that it occupies the site of Frogmoor Wharf and the premises of W. H. Walker, an important boatbuilding yard where many of the Grand Union Canal Carrying Company's carrying fleet were built. The first boats were built here in 1907, the last - the pair *Aberystwyth* and *Bangor* - in 1952. As well as GUCCC craft, Ovaltine and Cadbury had boats built by Walkers. In the 1930s, production was at the astonishing level of two wooden boats a week.

Out in open country, Stocker's Lock comes as a piquant reminder as to just how pretty a canal can be. The lock-keeper's cottage is particularly lovely, whilst, overlooking Bridge 175, stands Stocker's House, built for the collector of coal duties when the taxable boundary was moved closer to London than its original location north of Watford: a squat obelisk beside the towpath half a mile to the south marking the actual demarcation point itself. Stocker's Farm features a handsome cluster of weatherboarded barns which once appeared in a televised adaption of *Black Beauty*. Flooded gravel workings - now adapted for leisure use - and an abandoned chalk quarry, complete with loading chute and monkey (!), speak of lost industries. Still in business, though, as your nostrils may verify, is the giant sewage works at Maple Cross where a side-arm indicates that coal was once brought in by boat. Copper Mill Lock derives its name from the short-lived existence of a copper works beside the canal in the early years of the 19th century. Some interesting examples of industrial archaeology remain.

Map labels:

Ebury Way · 32 · A4145 · A404 · Canal Centre · 81 · Batchworth Lock · Rickmansworth · Town Centre · 173 6ft 8ins · Tesco · 174 · Aquadrome · mp · Stocker's Lake · Stocker's Lock · 82 5ft 2ins · 175 · Stockers Farm · A412 · disused chalk quarry · Springwell Lock · 83 · mp · 7ft 11ins · 176 · pipes · nature reserve · sewage works · Copper Mill Lock · 5ft 10ins · mp · 177 · 84 · Coy Carp · 70 · Troy Cut · Edwinns Brasserie · 178 · mp · 85 · Black Jack's Lock · 3ft 8ins · 179 · Wide Water Lock · 180 · 86 · 8ft 0ins · R. Colne · N

Harefield Marina · 34 · By-road to Denham

PLAYING 'kiss and tell' with the Colne, the Grand Union Canal makes its way through Denham Country Park before becoming embroiled in the suburban periphery of Uxbridge. These days, Harefield's flooded gravel pits are employed for the mooring of pleasure craft, but in 1958 they were the scene of mass scuttlings by the British Transport Commission of what, in their jaundiced perception - were unwonted and obsolete working narrowboats. Scandalised, the Inland Waterways Association likened Harefield Flash to Scapa Flow and embarrassed a flustered BTC to the extent that they denied that the deliberate sinkings had taken place.

A lengthy tree-lined straight is punctuated by an imposing blue-brick viaduct. A latecomer, in railway terms, it dates from the early 20th century, being constructed jointly by the Great Central and Great Western railway companies, the former to allay congestion on their shared line with the Metropolitan Railway, the latter to shorten their route to Birmingham. It is busy today with Chiltern Trains, unlike the branch line to Uxbridge High Street, closed to passenger trains in 1939.

Denham Deep, at just over eleven feet, lays claim to the greatest fall on the canal. Teas are obtainable here in idyllic surroundings, and days boats are for hire. The BTC may have thought, half a century ago, that canal trading had had its day, but they were myopically off-beam, for a new flow of aggregates began operating from a wharf beside Bridge 183 to a depot in West Drayton in 2003. A pair of purpose-built 90 tonne barges, named *Colne* and *Frays,* plus some tug-powered push-tows, ply back and forth with this traffic, a welcome reminder of the canal's original *raison d'etre* and an innovative way of keeping extra lorry movements off outer London's grid-locked roads. Further evidence of the canal's working past, as opposed to present, can be found by Bridge 186 where a boatyard occupies premises which once belonged to the famous canal carrying company Fellows, Morton & Clayton. Hillingdon Canal Club is located alongside.

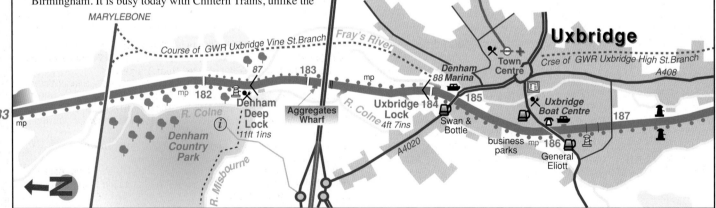

Aggregates barge on its way to West Drayton

Uxbridge

The most important town in the London Borough of Hillingdon, Uxbridge is a worthwhile stop on any boating itinerary. It was a Parliamentarian garrison town during the Civil War, and Charles I attempted to negotiate a peace treaty here in 1644. The Metropolitan Railway reached Uxbridge in 1904 followed by the Piccadilly Line in 1933, at which time the present handsome tube-train terminus was built. RAF Uxbridge opened in 1917 and Lawrence of Arabia passed through in the guise of Aircraftsman Ross. The Battle of Britain was directed from an underground command post at the aerodrome. Nowadays Uxbridge is a busy commercial centre and Brunel University has its home here.

FRAN'S TEA GARDEN - Denham Deep Lock. Tel: 01895 271070.
SOFRA - Rockingham Road. Tel: 01895 252248. Fabulous modern Turkish restaurant on way into town from Bridge 186.
NONNA ROSA III - High Street. Tel: 01895 255266. Very pleasant Italian restaurant & bar at north end of High Street.
GENERAL ELIOTT - adjacent Bridge 186. Tel: 01895 237385. Characterful canalside pub with terrace beside the towpath. Steaks a speciality.
SWAN & BOTTLE - canalside Bridge 185. Chef & Brewer restaurant/pub.

The much vaunted CHIMES and PAVILIONS shopping malls find their antithesis in Windsor Street, a quaint little throughfare of interesting shops, not least BARNARD'S BOOKSHOP.

COWLEY LOCK introduces a lengthy pound. If you're travelling towards central London there are no more locks to contend with you'll be relieved to learn. At Cowley Peachey Junction the Slough Arm slinks off on a five mile journey to the town which Betjeman would like to have bombed, a sequence of aqueducts carrying it unostentatiously through a bayou-like zone of water and wilderness. By Bridge 1 there's the dual interest of a pillbox and a coal tax obelisk.

Meanwhile the main line bears east, bisecting Yiewsley and West Drayton and running in close attendance with Brunel's Great Western Railway whose opening, in 1838, spelt the end of a hitherto successful packet boat operation between Uxbridge and Paddington. The broad gauge GWR's first pair of locomotives, *Vulcan* and *Premier* were built in Liverpool and brought by ship to London Docks before being floated up the canal to West Drayton. Along this length of canal once existed several arms to serve adjoining brickfields, a good example is still discernible by Bridge 195. Beware of (but also take time to admire) the aggregates barges discharging their cargoes by Bridge 196.

Map

- 188
- 34
- Malt Shovel
- Cowley Lock 6ft 6ins
- 89
- 70'
- B470
- 189
- Huntsmoor Park
- The Packet Boat
- Iver
- N
- The Water's Edge
- 190
- 70'
- A408
- Packet Boat Marina (BW) Alvechurch Boat Centres aqueducts
- COWLEY PEACHEY JUNCTION
- mp
- SLOUGH ARM
- 1
- M25
- R. Colne
- Fray's River
- Colne Brook
- 35A
- 3
- SLOUGH
- 2
- Iver
- 191
- 192
- West Drayton
- Yiewsley
- 193
- mp
- 94ft
- 194
- 195
- 196
- Business Park
- 198
- 197
- 199
- West Drayton
- A408
- Aggregates Depot
- 3
- PADDINGTON
- Railway to Heathrow

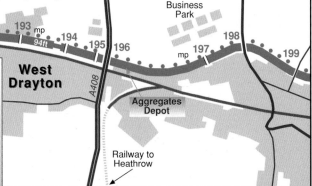

Summary of Facilities

MALT SHOVEL - canalside Bridge 188. Pleasantly refurbished all day pub. Tel: 01895 233121.

TOLL HOUSE TEAROOM - canalside Lock 89. Breakfasts, lunches, teas and takeaways - Tel: 01895 257940.

THE WATER'S EDGE - canalside Bridge 190. Restaurant and bar. Tel: 01895 440550.

PACKET BOAT - adjacent Bridge 190. CAMRA recommended pub with canal associations. Tel: 01895 442392.

Useful shops are handily placed at Yiewsley and accessible from Bridge 192. A large Co-op supermarket dominates, but there are many other retailers too, plus takeaways and sandwich bars.

* Allow 0.5 hours for this section of the Slough Arm

BRICKMAKING in the Slough area dates from the 15th century, when Henry VI had a kiln built to provide the bricks for Eton College, but the industry's zenith was in the second half of the 19th century and the Slough Arm - post-dating the parallel railway by fifty years - was built specifically to cater for this trade. Bricks were stacked all along the canal bank for loading on to barges and transporting to the construction sites of London's burgeoning suburbs. The brickmakers worked in teams of six and were paid piecework, around five shillings for every thousand bricks they made. It was seasonal work, summer only, and a beer allowance was a perk of the job, supplied to slake prodigious thirsts.

With its blue-brick overbridges, largely straight alignment, and absence of locks, the arm reminds you of the Cannock Extension Canal. It shares with that West Midland canal also, the distinction of a busy boatyard which, as far as Bridge 6 at any rate, brings considerable traffic to the canal. West of here, however, the arm has the character of a quiet backwater, the preserve of fishermen and model boat-builders keen to put their latest creations through their paces. Consequently, it is somewhat introspectively that the Slough Arm moves towards its undemonstrative terminus. Airliners flying in and out of Heathrow provide an aural and aerial backdrop to the proceedings. During the summer months the display of water lilies in the margins of the canal would do justice to an ornamental water garden, though their mere presence emphasises the shallow, unboated nature of the canal.

Five miles from Cowley Peachey the arm peters out by a builders merchant's yard, the best part of a mile north of Slough's town centre. It is surprising and regrettable that the opportunity was not taken in the first half of the 20th century to extend the canal into Slough's famous trading estate where new traffics may have been won to prolong transport by water in the London area. In the event the western extremity of the Slough Arm slumbers on as the sort of route you cruise simply to say that you have done so, and, pending rumours of redevelopment materialising, the terminal basin wears the apologetic air of a late birthday present.

High Line Yachting

Slough

The town centre lies a quarter of an hour's dispiriting walk south of the canal, though there are suburban facilities on the way. The station is a fine example of railway architecture. Beyond the underpass, the Queensmere and Observatory shopping precincts cater for most aspects of modern life, the latter drawing its name from Slough's associations with the 18th century astronomer, William Herschel. But the best thing about the town today is its MUSEUM at the eastern end of the High Street. Open Wednesday to Saturday between 11.30am and 4pm, it pays tribute to Slough's lively past - Tel: 01753 526422.

EXPLORING London's present day canal system, yet remaining ignorant of the trades and traffics of its past, is as inexcusable as visiting Flanders and not being aware of its role in two world wars. By all means enjoy the present, but learn to savour those clues which remain to a busier past. Nestle's factory was known to generations of working boatmen as 'Hayes Cocoa' (mooring rings remain embedded in the concrete dock), Kearley & Tonge's nearby preserves factory, 'The Jam 'Ole'; at Bulls Bridge there were maintenance docks, a traffic control office, and a long lay-by provided for boats and their crews awaiting orders for their next cargo. Somehow the residential boats which fill the lay-by now, eclectic in function and style as they are (some even running to two storeys), seem a poor substitute for pairs of working boats.

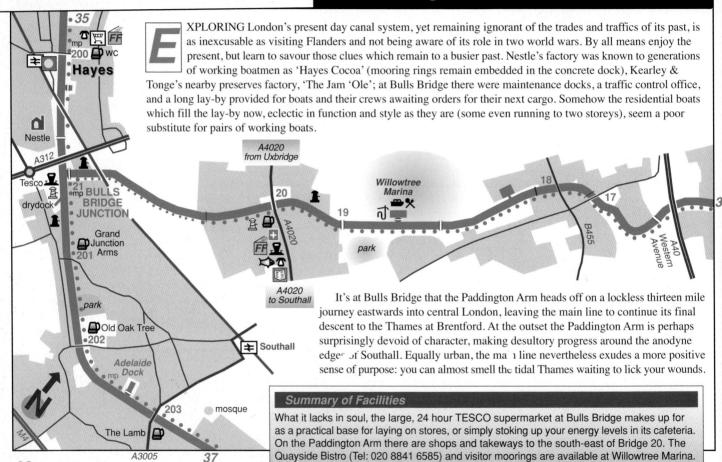

It's at Bulls Bridge that the Paddington Arm heads off on a lockless thirteen mile journey eastwards into central London, leaving the main line to continue its final descent to the Thames at Brentford. At the outset the Paddington Arm is perhaps surprisingly devoid of character, making desultory progress around the anodyne edges of Southall. Equally urban, the main line nevertheless exudes a more positive sense of purpose: you can almost smell the tidal Thames waiting to lick your wounds.

Summary of Facilities

What it lacks in soul, the large, 24 hour TESCO supermarket at Bulls Bridge makes up for as a practical base for laying on stores, or simply stoking up your energy levels in its cafeteria. On the Paddington Arm there are shops and takeways to the south-east of Bridge 20. The Quayside Bistro (Tel: 020 8841 6585) and visitor moorings are available at Willowtree Marina.

*Figures refer to main line, allow 1 hour for Paddington Arm between Bulls Bridge and Western Avenue.

Picnic on the Paddington Arm or Homage to Cartier-Bresson.

37 GRAND UNION CANAL

Hanwell & Brentford 4mls/12lks/3hrs

A dozen locks carry the canal down into the valley of the Brent and on to join the Thames. This is an especially enjoyable and interesting section of canal to explore. Above Norwood Top Lock an arm built to serve a margarine factory remains in water; it also saw use by a company engaged in the distribution of tinned sardines. At Three Bridges a road crosses the canal simultaneously as the canal crosses a railway. It was apparently one of Isambard Kingdom Brunel's last engineering projects and brings to mind a similar sequence of structures - rail over road over river - at Struan on the Highland Railway's main line north of Blair Atholl.

Closely spaced, locks 92-97 were known to working boatmen as the 'Thick of Hanwell'. They are overlooked by the grim facade of a Victorian mental asylum once served by an arched loading bay whose infilled brickwork can still be discerned. The Hanwell flight has side ponds which British Waterways are considering restoring. Three attractive lock-keepers cottages overlook the flight.

John Betjeman's 'gentle Brent' enters the canal at the tail of Lock 97. Occasionally its current belies his poetry and makes steering a job deserving of full concentration. Between Bridge 205A and Osterley Lock an old plaque proudly recalls that this length won a pile-driving competition in 1959!

Despite being surrounded by urbanisation, the canal has its rural moments, fringed by reed and balsam and shaded by alder and willow. Bridge 207 is a graceful cast iron structure known as Gallows Bridge, bearing its place and date of manufacture, Horseley Iron Works near Birmingham 1820.

Both the M4 motorway and the Piccadilly Line cross the canal before it makes its way into Brentford past big silvery office blocks and under the London & South Western Railway's Hounslow Loop. The Great Western Railway's branch down to Brentford from Southall lost its passenger services during the Second World War, but remains used by trains carrying

PUTNEY
36
HOUNSLOW
River Thames from Reading

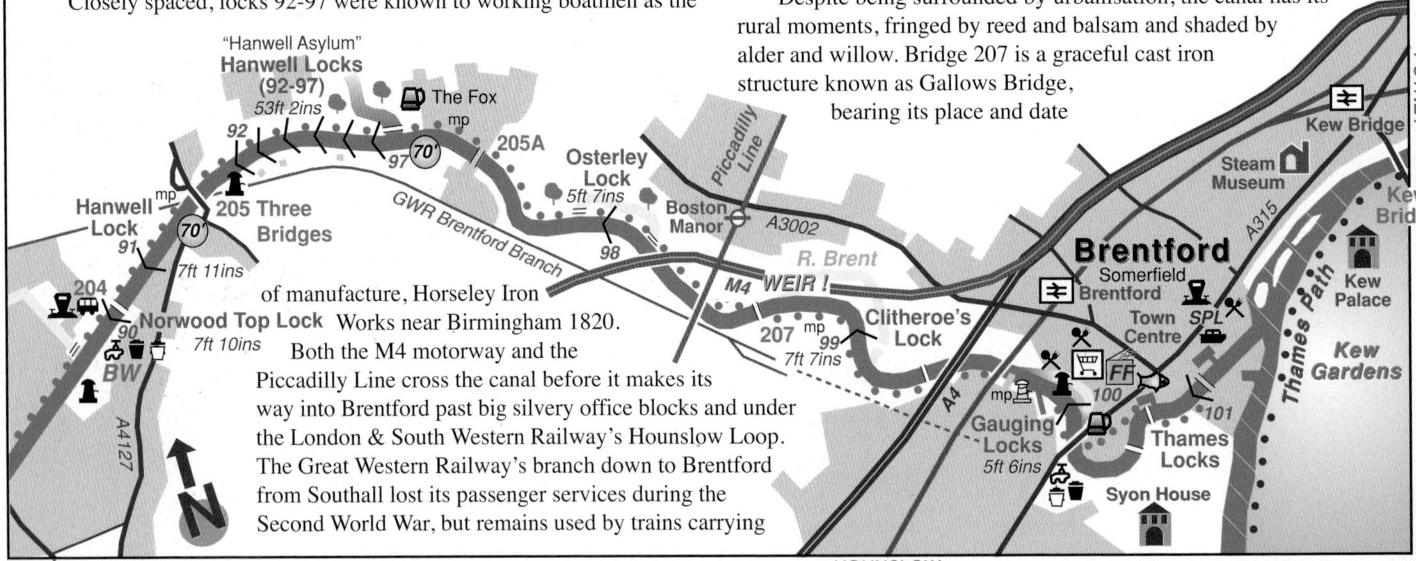

refuse to a landfill site near Didcot in Oxfordshire.

A huge empty warehouse overhangs the canal and its towpath, reproachfully contrasting with a redevelopment zone of smart apartments (pseudo-romantically known as Heron View and The Island) as if to say 'I am a remnant from a time when this canal worked for its living, you are merely brash upstarts'. Here, moored for up to a fortnight at Visitor Moorings designated by British Waterways, the more imaginative of boat crews can fantasize that they work for Willow Wren, and that any moment Leslie Morton will appear on the towpath bearing orders for them to load wheat for Wellingborough or timber for Tipton.

Beyond the moorings, the duplicated (side by side) Gauging Locks are incongruously overlooked by a Holiday Inn, a far cry from the days when Thames lighters would tranship their cargoes into narrowboats in what was once a vibrant dockland setting. Electrically operated (with a boaters key) these locks and the following pair of Thames Locks mark the end of the canal's long journey from the Midlands. Boaters proceeding down on to the Thames are recommended to consult the Inland Waterways Association's *Thames Tideway Guide* - Tel: 01923 711114 for details of how to acquire a copy. The telephone number for Thames Locks is 020 8568 2779. For exploration of the Thames by boat we recommend Chris Cove-Smith's *River Thames Book* published by Imray.

Brentford

Though redevelopment marches remorselessly on, pockets of old Brentford (such as the charming Butts behind the Market Place) remain, establishing a characterful conclusion to your voyage down from the midlands.

THE WEIR - Market Place. Tel: 020 8568 3600. Formerly a street corner pub called The White Horse, this is now a sophisticated bar and eating place with a fine garden backing on to the River Brent. Fascinatingly, the artist Turner stayed here as a boy circa 1785.

LA ROSETTA - High Street. Tel: 020 8560 3002. Italian.

MAGPIE & CROWN - High Street. Tel: 020 8560 5658. Lively 'dockland' local recommended in the Good Beer Guide, notable for its choice of real ales and Continental beers on draught.

THE FOX - adjacent foot of Hanwell flight. Tel: 020 8567 3912. Unspoilt pub with a big garden. Also fish & chips, takeaways and sandwich shops along the High Street 3 minutes walk from the Gauging Locks.

All facilities in the High Street, including a branch of Somerfield and launderette.

KEW BRIDGE STEAM MUSEUM - Green Dragon Lane. Tel: 020 8568 4757. Superb museum housed in 19th century waterworks dominated by ornate tower chimney.

TRAINS - frequent services to/from London Waterloo and Windsor. Tel: 08457 484950. BUSES - easy access to/from central London Tel: 020 7222 1234.

Gallows Bridge

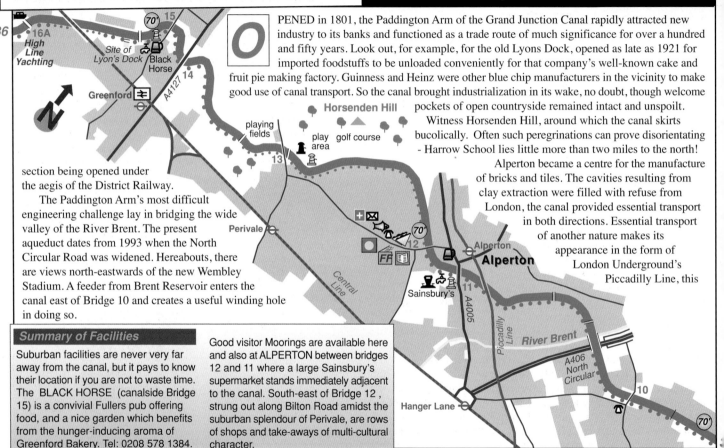

O PENED in 1801, the Paddington Arm of the Grand Junction Canal rapidly attracted new industry to its banks and functioned as a trade route of much significance for over a hundred and fifty years. Look out, for example, for the old Lyons Dock, opened as late as 1921 for imported foodstuffs to be unloaded conveniently for that company's well-known cake and fruit pie making factory. Guinness and Heinz were other blue chip manufacturers in the vicinity to make good use of canal transport. So the canal brought industrialization in its wake, no doubt, though welcome pockets of open countryside remained intact and unspoilt.

Witness Horsenden Hill, around which the canal skirts bucolically. Often such peregrinations can prove disorientating - Harrow School lies little more than two miles to the north! Alperton became a centre for the manufacture of bricks and tiles. The cavities resulting from clay extraction were filled with refuse from London, the canal provided essential transport in both directions. Essential transport of another nature makes its appearance in the form of London Underground's Piccadilly Line, this

section being opened under the aegis of the District Railway.

The Paddington Arm's most difficult engineering challenge lay in bridging the wide valley of the River Brent. The present aqueduct dates from 1993 when the North Circular Road was widened. Hereabouts, there are views north-eastwards of the new Wembley Stadium. A feeder from Brent Reservoir enters the canal east of Bridge 10 and creates a useful winding hole in doing so.

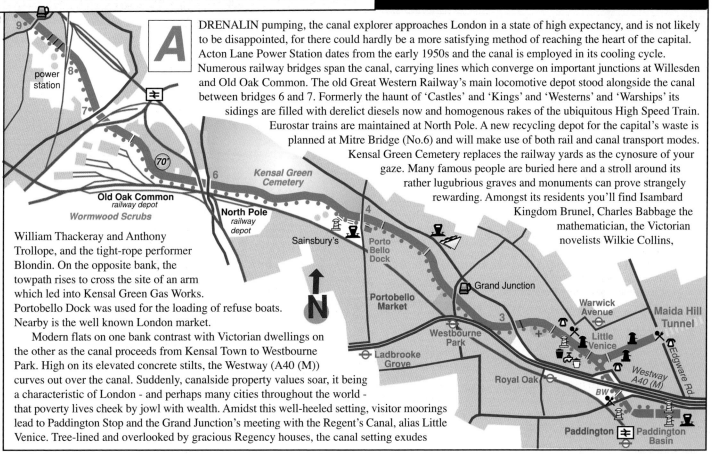

A DRENALIN pumping, the canal explorer approaches London in a state of high expectancy, and is not likely to be disappointed, for there could hardly be a more satisfying method of reaching the heart of the capital. Acton Lane Power Station dates from the early 1950s and the canal is employed in its cooling cycle. Numerous railway bridges span the canal, carrying lines which converge on important junctions at Willesden and Old Oak Common. The old Great Western Railway's main locomotive depot stood alongside the canal between bridges 6 and 7. Formerly the haunt of 'Castles' and 'Kings' and 'Westerns' and 'Warships' its sidings are filled with derelict diesels now and homogenous rakes of the ubiquitous High Speed Train. Eurostar trains are maintained at North Pole. A new recycling depot for the capital's waste is planned at Mitre Bridge (No.6) and will make use of both rail and canal transport modes. Kensal Green Cemetery replaces the railway yards as the cynosure of your gaze. Many famous people are buried here and a stroll around its rather lugubrious graves and monuments can prove strangely rewarding. Amongst its residents you'll find Isambard Kingdom Brunel, Charles Babbage the mathematician, the Victorian novelists Wilkie Collins,

William Thackeray and Anthony Trollope, and the tight-rope performer Blondin. On the opposite bank, the towpath rises to cross the site of an arm which led into Kensal Green Gas Works. Portobello Dock was used for the loading of refuse boats. Nearby is the well known London market.

Modern flats on one bank contrast with Victorian dwellings on the other as the canal proceeds from Kensal Town to Westbourne Park. High on its elevated concrete stilts, the Westway (A40 (M)) curves out over the canal. Suddenly, canalside property values soar, it being a characteristic of London - and perhaps many cities throughout the world - that poverty lives cheek by jowl with wealth. Amidst this well-heeled setting, visitor moorings lead to Paddington Stop and the Grand Junction's meeting with the Regent's Canal, alias Little Venice. Tree-lined and overlooked by gracious Regency houses, the canal setting exudes exceptional charm. Residential moorings provide the opportunity to enjoy an enviable amphibious lifestyle in central London, whilst the canal setting attracts large numbers of visitors who perhaps subconsciously perceive the canal as a potential escape route from the pressures of everyday urban existence, even if they get no further than a trip to Camden Lock.

Framed by Maida Avenue and Blomfield Road (where the novelist and early IWA secretary, Elizabeth Jane Howard, once lived) the Regent's Canal leaves Little Venice via the shadowy portal of Maida Hill Tunnel on its way to meet the Thames at Limehouse. The Paddington Arm, on the other hand, makes a dog-leg turn into its wide terminal basin, recently redeveloped to good effect with some excellent Visitor Moorings provided in the shadow of St Mary's famous hospital.

Paddington

All London lies at your feet, and even Pearson's, usually so comprehensive, so trustworthy, so inspirational, demur from attempting to spell it out for you. The secret is, not to attempt *too* much; assimilate London in postal districts, and you won't be overawed. The BIG BUS COMPANY (Tel: 020 7233 9533) operate open top sight-seeing tours from Paddington which form an ideal introduction to the capital.

JASON'S - canalside, Blomfield Road, Little Venice. Tel: 020 7286 6752. Eat exceedingly well and watch the boats go by. WATERSIDE CAFE - Little Venice. Tel: 020 7266 1066. Light snacks on board this cafe boat or at adjoining towpath tables. THE UNION - Sheldon Square. Tel: 020 7289 3063. Stylish modern bar/restaurant alongside the arm leading into Paddington Basin. ABERDEEN STEAK HOUSE - Praed Street. Tel: 020 7724 4874. Big steaks for hungry boaters amidst 'very Sixties' surroundings opposite Paddington station.

A handy TESCO EXPRESS can be found at the furthest end of Paddington Basin. Similarly, there's a BUDGENS convenience outlet opposite Paddington station on Praed Street. Otherwise you'll just have to hoof it to Harrods or Fortnum & Masons. To make yourself presentable in the eyes of such august establishments doormen, there's a useful launderette on nearby London Street.

TOURIST INFORMATION - Tel: 09068 663344 or visit *www.visitlondon.com*

BUSES/UNDERGROUND - Tel: 020 7222 1234.TRAINS - Tel: 08457 484950.

Kensal Green

Paddington Basin

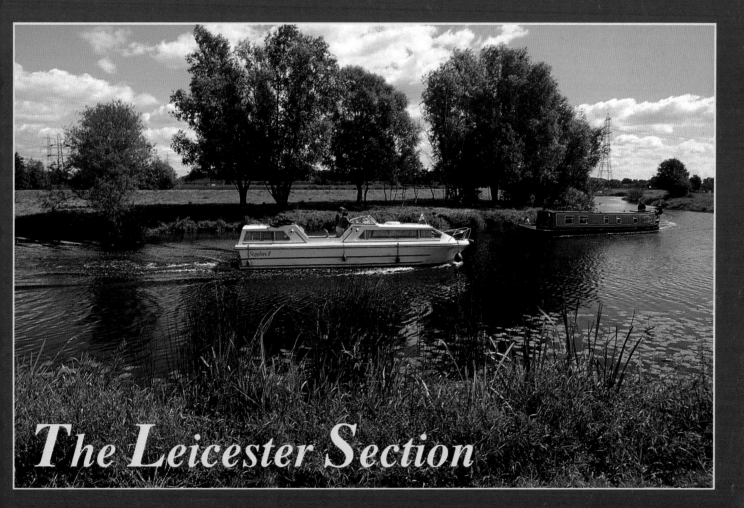

The Leicester Section

SILLITOE'S early novel springs to mind, retitled *The Loneliness of the Long Distance Boater*, as you assuredly come to terms with the Leicester Section's remote atmosphere. Canal, railway, and two generations of main road plunge through a gap in the hills between the villages of Ashby St Ledgers and Watford. By now you will be beginning to realise that you get nowhere fast on this stretch of canal, but as there isn't anywhere particular to go, this barely seems to matter. The bridge which carries the West Coast Main Line over the canal repays a second glance, being curiously constructed with barrel vaulting at ninety degrees to the waterway rather than the forty-five degree angle suggested by the configuration of the railway.Presumably it was Robert Stephenson's work, the classical decoration of the ironwork girders and railings certainly bears his hallmark. Welton station, just to the north of the canal bridge, closed in 1958, though its redbrick goods shed remains intact as is so often the case, still usefully storing something, even if its awning looks as though it will soon abandon the fight against gravity.

Boats coagulate at WATFORD LOCKS like parties of ramblers queuing to climb a stile. Happily you are no longer expected to fathom their complex operation - which ran to three pages of text in the early British Waterways guides - rather you are encouraged to make the lock-keeper aware of your presence and he or she will guide you through the flight's devilish machinations.

Watford Locks raise the canal to its summit level of 412 feet. At the turn of the century there were plans to replace the flight with an inclined plane like that at Foxton, but the scheme was shelved. When the Grand Union was formed in 1929 there were further proposals for the flight to be widened, but these also languished. Above the locks - once you are clear of the M1 - the Leicester Section quickly establishes its reclusive character, painfully shy of encounters with villages. The first time we came this way we ran out of food and money! CRICK TUNNEL is almost a mile long and, in common with the other two tunnels on the route, doesn't have a towpath. In the old days boat horses found their way over the top via Watford Road and Boathorse Lane, the way that walkers have still to trudge today.

Watford

An extremely pretty estate village which has somehow survived the building of the M1 past its back door. There's no shop now, but in extremis you can find your way surreptitiously from Bridge 6 to the adjacent motorway services. THE THAI GARDEN by Bridge 6 brings the taste of the Orient to rural Northants. - Tel: 01327 703621.

Crick

Useful watering-hole on the Rugby-Northampton road. Post office stores adjacent to Bridge 12 and a Co-op deeper into the village. Three pubs in the centre, but we'd recommend EDWARDS, a comfortable canalside restaurant offering morning coffee up until noon, an imaginative lunch menu thereafter, and similarly dinner too; "traditional English and French cooking with fresh local ingredients given a modern twist" in the words of the husband and wife owners. Tel: 01788 822517.

CRICK TUNNEL
1528 yards

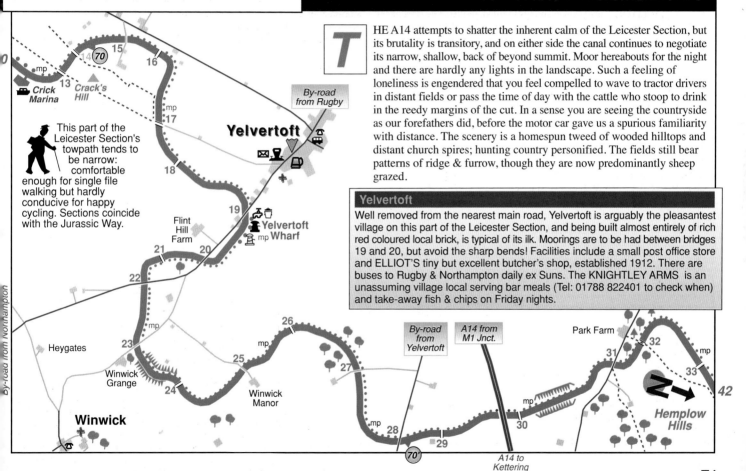

THE A14 attempts to shatter the inherent calm of the Leicester Section, but its brutality is transitory, and on either side the canal continues to negotiate its narrow, shallow, back of beyond summit. Moor hereabouts for the night and there are hardly any lights in the landscape. Such a feeling of loneliness is engendered that you feel compelled to wave to tractor drivers in distant fields or pass the time of day with the cattle who stoop to drink in the reedy margins of the cut. In a sense you are seeing the countryside as our forefathers did, before the motor car gave us a spurious familiarity with distance. The scenery is a homespun tweed of wooded hilltops and distant church spires; hunting country personified. The fields still bear patterns of ridge & furrow, though they are now predominantly sheep grazed.

Yelvertoft

Well removed from the nearest main road, Yelvertoft is arguably the pleasantest village on this part of the Leicester Section, and being built almost entirely of rich red coloured local brick, is typical of its ilk. Moorings are to be had between bridges 19 and 20, but avoid the sharp bends! Facilities include a small post office store and ELLIOT'S tiny but excellent butcher's shop, established 1912. There are buses to Rugby & Northampton daily ex Suns. The KNIGHTLEY ARMS is an unassuming village local serving bar meals (Tel: 01788 822401 to check when) and take-away fish & chips on Friday nights.

This part of the Leicester Section's towpath tends to be narrow: comfortable enough for single file walking but hardly conducive for happy cycling. Sections coincide with the Jurassic Way.

Crick Marina
Crack's Hill
By-road from Rugby
Yelvertoft
Flint Hill Farm
Yelvertoft Wharf
Heygates
Winwick Grange
Winwick
Winwick Manor
By-road from Yelvertoft
A14 from M1 Jnct.
Park Farm
Hemplow Hills
A14 to Kettering
By-road from Northampton

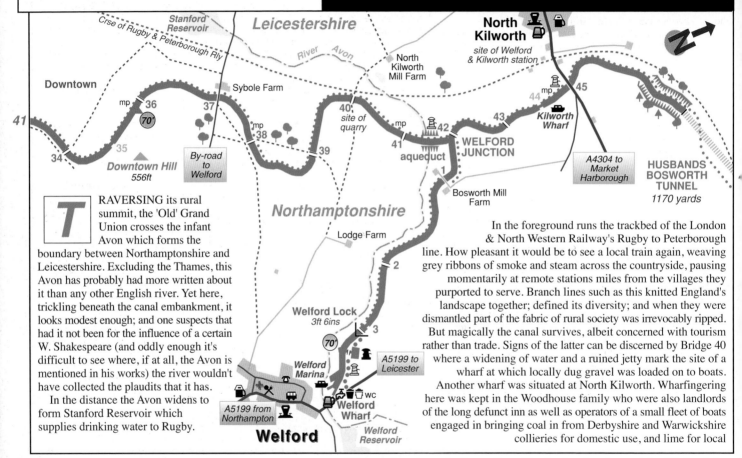

TRAVERSING its rural summit, the 'Old' Grand Union crosses the infant Avon which forms the boundary between Northamptonshire and Leicestershire. Excluding the Thames, this Avon has probably had more written about it than any other English river. Yet here, trickling beneath the canal embankment, it looks modest enough; and one suspects that had it not been for the influence of a certain W. Shakespeare (and oddly enough it's difficult to see where, if at all, the Avon is mentioned in his works) the river wouldn't have collected the plaudits that it has.

In the distance the Avon widens to form Stanford Reservoir which supplies drinking water to Rugby.

In the foreground runs the trackbed of the London & North Western Railway's Rugby to Peterborough line. How pleasant it would be to see a local train again, weaving grey ribbons of smoke and steam across the countryside, pausing momentarily at remote stations miles from the villages they purported to serve. Branch lines such as this knitted England's landscape together; defined its diversity; and when they were dismantled part of the fabric of rural society was irrevocably ripped. But magically the canal survives, albeit concerned with tourism rather than trade. Signs of the latter can be discerned by Bridge 40 where a widening of water and a ruined jetty mark the site of a wharf at which locally dug gravel was loaded on to boats. Another wharf was situated at North Kilworth. Wharfingering here was kept in the Woodhouse family who were also landlords of the long defunct inn as well as operators of a small fleet of boats engaged in bringing coal in from Derbyshire and Warwickshire collieries for domestic use, and lime for local

*Time refers to main line, allow 45 minutes (each way) for Welford Arm

agriculture. Apparently one of the Woodhouse boats was contracted to carry scrap when the inclined plane at Foxton was being demolished, but its back was broken under the weight of the load and it sank at the foot of the flight. L.T.C. Rolt mentioned the family's pub in *Narrow Boat*. North of the wharf the canal winds through a deep, tree-bowered cutting to the portal of Husbands Bosworth Tunnel.

The Welford Arm

Not so much an arm, more a finger, this branch was dug to bring water from Welford, Sulby and Naseby reservoirs to feed the main line. But a certain amount of trade developed, and coal was still being brought to Welford by boat at the end of the Second World War. Thereafter the arm fell into decay - though retaining its role as a feeder - and was allowed to silt up. It remained unnavigable for twenty years until its re-opening in 1969.

Leaving the main line, the arm establishes its individuality by dint of its overbridges being numbered from one upwards. Furthermore, the adjacent ridges close in to create a feeling of intimacy in contrast with the panoramic views offered by the rest of the Leicester Section. After a mile the arm rises through a diminutive lock to reach the highest pound on the whole of the former Grand Union system. The terminus is just around the corner, and the arm's deceptive calm is exposed as an illusion by the density of boats moored in two lagoons.

A detour up the Welford Arm is difficult to resist. Boaters are, by definition, explorers at heart, and the end of the arm makes a pleasant overnight mooring with the facilities of the village and the wildlife of the reservoirs near at hand. The country writer 'BB' (alias Denys Watkins-Pitchford, who illustrated *Narrow Boat*) included several passages describing the flora and fauna of the Welford Arm in his book *The Wayfaring Tree*.

Welford

One of two villages with the same name on the Warwickshire Avon, this Welford straddles the old A50 (now A5199), a road which wandered its way from Northampton to Warrington via Leicester and Stoke-on-Trent, crossing a fair few canals in its path. The village itself features many attractive vernacular houses, characteristically of redbrick and thatch. Three miles to the east lies Naseby, scene, in 1645, of the decisive battle of the Civil War. Nearer at hand a public footpath bisects the canal feeder reservoirs of Welford and Sulby.

WHARF INN - canalside at terminus. Tel: 01858 575075. Pleasant pub - the only one left in the village now - offering bar and restaurant food, plus accommodation.

ELIZABETHAN RESTAURANT - High Street. Tel: 01858 575311. Long-established restaurant which has gone through many guises, now promoted as a 'country pub & restaurant' offering dinner dances and theme nights.

Mace post office stores and newsagency on High Street open daily early to late.

BUSES - Stagecoach services to/from Market Harborough (via Husbands Bosworth) and Northampton. Not Sundays. Tel: 0870 608 2 608.

North Kilworth

Sadly, there are too many lorries using the main road to make the walk into North Kilworth pleasurable for those off the canal. A disappointment, because a locally-produced Historic Village Trail leaflet suggests that there are many points of interest.

The leaflet also includes the sorry tale of a Kilworth woman whose German husband was interned during the Second World War and her Alsation dog shot by the village policeman, simply because it was a German Shepherd.

Cruising under the Laughton Hills

KEEPING to a contour 412 feet above sea level, the canal spans the watershed between the Welland and the Avon, disdaining locks but having no alternative other than to penetrate the hill at Husbands Bosworth by way of a lengthy tunnel. The landscape is gorgeously typical of The Shires, consisting of broad, high hedged pastures interspersed with fox coverts, spinneys and substantial houses erected as hunting lodges by the fox and hounds brigade. One such is Lubenham Lodge, adjacent to Bridge 58. Sheltered by tall pines and chestnuts, the property evokes a sense of timeless, gracious living and well-being. Its dormer windows must offer a peerless prospect over the Vale of Welland. Nearby, the Laughton Hills spill down from five hundred feet or so to the water's edge in a series of lush, velvety folds. Mile after ravishing mile the countryside unrolls its beauty for the benefit of the canal traveller, invoking a sense of well-being whatever the weather. Solely mileposts and bridge numbers register movement, otherwise you

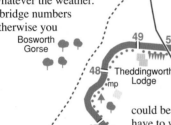

could be forgiven for thinking that you are in some extraordinary sort of trance. Pedestrians have to walk over the top of Husbands Bosworth Tunnel, but it is a thoroughly enjoyable detour encountering, en route, a graceful occupation bridge across the grassy trackbed of the dismantled railway. The bosky, musky horse-path can get a little overgrown during the summer months - though nothing that the practised country walker can't deal with. Elsewhere the towpath - framed by a shade-providing hedge of considerable height - is fine for single-file pedestrians, but protruding roots and pockets of erosion render it impraticable for cycling.

Husbands Bosworth

Husbands Bosworth acquired its prefix in the 17th century in deference to Market Bosworth, twenty miles to the north-west. It is a sizeable village of winding lanes (one called Honeypot) embracing predominantly brick houses of much charm. However, in our experience mooring is a tad difficult by Bridge 46 where the cutting restricts channel width and lack of depth makes it difficult to get as close to the bank as you'd like. Nevertheless, facilities include a pub, a charmingly old-fashioned general store, and newsagent/ post office. Buses run hourly Mon-Sat to Market Harborough and Hinckley - Tel: 0870 608 2 608.

LEICESTERSHIRE folk seem to regard FOXTON LOCKS as their own personal street-theatre. They descend on the famous flight in droves. Leaving their vehicles in the car park at the top, they stroll down to the pub, giving scant rein to their children's excitement, much to the chagrin of the lock-keeper who lives with perpetual fear of tragedy. The inland navigator plays a walk on part in Foxton's soap opera, and is expected to respond cheerfully to bizarre questions and fatuous remarks with the amused tolerance of a Gulliver amidst Lilliputians. That Foxton is a canal centre at all is due to historical accident. The original concept, dating from 1793, was for a canal to link Leicester with Northampton; connection southwards with the Grand Junction Canal would be made at the latter town. In the event, the Leicestershire

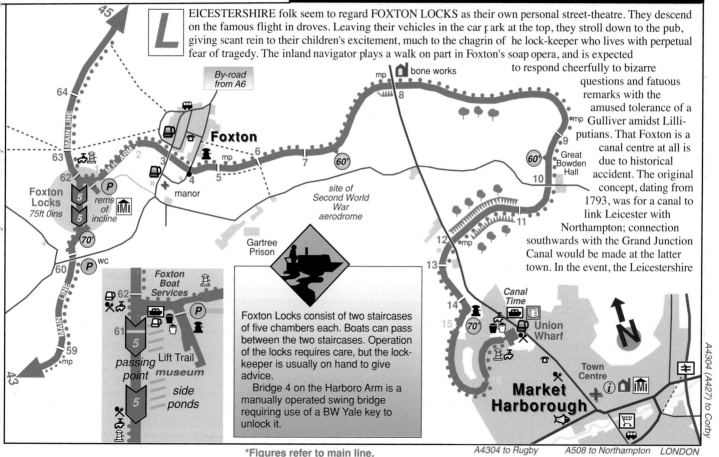

Foxton Locks consist of two staircases of five chambers each. Boats can pass between the two staircases. Operation of the locks requires care, but the lock-keeper is usually on hand to give advice.

Bridge 4 on the Harboro Arm is a manually operated swing bridge requiring use of a BW Yale key to unlock it.

*Figures refer to main line, allow 2 hours for Harboro Arm

& Northamptonshire Union Canal - built to broadbeam dimensions - ran out of capital and was forced to terminate for a dozen ignominious years at the village of Debdale (Map 45). Progress southwards as far as Market Harborough was completed in 1809, but the direct route to Northampton was never built. In exasperation, a new company was promoted to link the Leics & Northants with the Grand Junction. Known as the 'Grand Union', it charted a 23-mile route from Norton to Foxton including two precipitous flights of narrowbeam locks at either end of the twenty mile summit.

Thus the seeds were sown for Foxton's prominence. The village that had never been earmarked as a junction settled down to three-quarters of a century of fluctuating trade. The 'Grand Union' never made much profit and was bought out by the Grand Junction in 1894. Fellows, Morton & Clayton, the route's prime users, were by this time agitating for improvements to the bottle-neck staircases at Watford and Foxton and for a widening of the gauge. In what, with hindsight, can be seen as an over-enthusiastic response, the Grand Junction proposed boat lifts, or more properly, inclined planes, at both sites. Only the one at Foxton was built, it opened in 1900. Archive photographs reveal the astonishing grandeur of the inclined plane: an upper and lower dock, separated by a 1:4 gradient laid with rails, supporting two counterbalanced tanks each capable of taking a barge or pair of narrowboats. In the extremely informative booklet describing the plane, its history and operation, and admirable plans for restoration, the Foxton Inclined Plane Trust describe an imaginary journey through the lift; a ten minute ride replacing an hour on the locks. As an experience it must have been like travelling in a huge, open air funicular.

But for all their tub-thumping, FMC's trade never built to a level commensurate with the viable operation of the lift. Days were wont to go by when the attendants had nothing better to do than stoke the boiler and squirt oil on the moving parts: the railways had long since cornered the bulk of traffic between the East Midlands and London. Paradoxically, FMC and other carriers were irked that the lift was closed at night, occasioning delay to the 24 hour 'fly' boats which used the route. In response, the locks - unused since the opening of the lift - were reinstated and, inevitably, it was not long before these were deemed economically preferable to the lift, closure of which is recorded as having taken place in November 1910. The structure lay derelict through the years of the First World War, but was demolished in 1928 by a firm of Shropshire scrap merchants, who paid a paltry £250 for the privilege.

The Market Harborough Arm

The scheme for a through route to Northampton moribund, the canal between Foxton and Market Harborough lapsed into branch status, a character prevalent to this day. Busier since Canal Time established themselves in the revitalised terminal basin, the arm still tends to attract the sort of boaters who are never happier than when poking their inquisitive prows up the lonely backwaters of the system. The arm circles the skirts of Gallows Hill. To the north-east there are splendid vistas across the village-sprinkled valley of the River Welland. During the Second World War they built a bomber base on the top of Gallow Hill on a site now occupied by Gartree Prison, a maximum security establishment whose high walls and floodlights can occasionally be glimpsed from the canal. Some years ago a prisoner made a daring escape in a helicopter flown into the prison compound by an accomplice.

By Bridge 8 there is a factory engaged in the unsavoury and occasionally noxious business of transforming old animal bones into meal and tallow for use in the manufacture (elsewhere) of animal feeds and soap. Otherwise, the arm is largely undisturbed and undemonstrative, fringed with reeds, arrowhead and water lilies, its narrow channel measured, mile by mile, with the aid of simple iron mileposts counting the distance from Foxton.

Practically boxing the compass, the arm's entrance into Market Harborough is abruptly suburban - all lawns, laurels and lachrymose willows. The terminal basin looks exemplary these days, though it seems unfair that visiting boaters have to moor outside its historic confines unless they ask at the boatyard and pay a small fee. After all, this was the scene in 1950 of the fledgling Inland Waterways Association's first festival. It proved a resounding success, even though the Association was being torn apart by a deep schism between its two chief founders, Robert Aickman and Tom Rolt. Over a hundred boats attended and fifty thousand visitors enjoyed the festival's mixture of canal exhibits and theatrical entertainment. One imagines that the whole event would have made a marvellous film subject for an Ealing Comedy. Perhaps the ghosts of Rolt and Aickman, still at loggerheads, will disturb your sleep with their bickering ...

Foxton

Foxton village basks in the sun like a sleek cat that has just had two helpings of cream. Property prices here must average six figures, and on weekdays when the bread-winners are away it is as quiet as a nunnery. Up on their hilltop, the manor and the church daydream of a feudal past. All too predictably, there hasn't been a shop in the village for a number of years (the last one in use has become the premises of a pre-school group) but basic provisions are obtainable from the canal shop at the foot of the locks.

FOXTON LOCKS INN - canalside bottom lock. First of the Waterside Pub Partnership chain, offers 'a range of menus from morning coffee and pastries, tapas, light lunches, afternoon teas, through to an evening a la carte menu'. Tel: 0116 279 1515.

BRIDGE 61 - canalside bottom lock. Cosy antidote to Foxton Locks Inn. Light snacks and real ale. Tel: 0116 279 2285.

BLACK HORSE - adjacent Bridge 3. Welcoming Greene King pub with conservatory restaurant and lovely garden overlooked by village church. Tel: 0116 545250.

There are cafes at the top and bottom of the locks pandering to the busy traffic in gongoozlers. Laundry facilities are available from Foxton Boat Services.

LIFT TRAIL & MUSEUM - waymarked path around the site of the inclined plane and interesting exhibits in the former boiler house. Tel: 0116 279 2657.

BOAT TRIPS - short horse-drawn trips on Sundays and Bank Hols. Tel: 0116 279 2285.

BRITISH WATERWAYS organise a lively programme of events based on Foxton Locks. For further details telephone 01908 302500 or visit the website *www.foxtonlocks.com*

BUSES - Tel: 0870 608 2 608. Hourly Mon-Sat service to/from Market Harborough and Fleckney offers the chance for a one-way walk along the Market Harborough Arm or northwards along the main line.

Market Harborough

Watered by the River Welland, Market Harborough is an inherently good looking town, exuding a healthy vitality without being too self-consciously touristy. Archive photographs in the bar of the Three Swans hotel depict the High Street early in the 20th century with the cattle market in full swing. Building of the A6 by-pass a few years back hasn't quite returned the town to such bucolic scenes, but one welcomes some degree of hustle and bustle as a palliative to the soporific charm of the Leicester Section. Here and there stand some charming architectural oddities. Take, for example, Church Square, dominated by the parish church of St Dionysius with its soaring ashlar spire, but also the location of a wonderfully picturesque timber building on stilts that was formerly the grammar school and a handsome textile mill (Symington's corset factory) which looks as though it has surreptitiously travelled down the A6 from Stockport. In fact there were two strands to the Symington family, Scots brothers who arrived in the town in 1827. James Symington married a stay maker and never looked back - in their 20th century heyday Symingtons were innovators of the Liberty Bodice. William Symington turned his talents to food production and the company's name became synonymous with pea soup and table cream.

COVATIS - Union Wharf. Marvellous Italian restaurant located in the former Terminal Warehouse with tables spilling out on to the quayside itself in the summer months. Tel: 01858 468100.

JOULE'S EATING HOUSE - off High Street. Splendid wholefood annex to Joule's clothing store. Al fresco dining on hot days. Tel: 01858 463250.

THE THREE SWANS - High Street. Best Western hotel once famous for belonging to the eccentric inn-keeper John Fothergill who wrote about it in his book *My Three Inns*. Also referred to by Robert Aickman (founder of the IWA) in his description of the first National Rally in *The River Runs Uphill*. Bar and restaurant meals and a handsome wrought-iron sign depicting the three swans hanging out over the High Street. Tel: 01858 466644.

ASCOUGH'S - High Street. Good value bistro. Tel: 01858 466966.

There are Sainsbury, Tesco and Co-op supermarkets. The market hall (down by the lugubrious banks of the River Welland) operates on Tuesdays, Fridays and Saturdays and there's a Farmer's Market held in the Square on the first Thursday in the month. Elsewhere, there are some charmingly individual retailers like BATES the butcher, HOBBS the fishmonger and DUNCAN MURRAY the wine merchants, plus a nice little bookshop called QUINNS in the same alley as Joule's Eating House.

TOURIST INFORMATION - The Library, Adam & Eve Street. Tel: 01858 828282 *www.harboroughonline.co.uk* Housed in Symington's former corset factory which also contains (around the back!) HARBOROUGH MUSEUM an interesting display of the town's past. Tel: 01858 821085.

TRAINS - Midland Mainline to/from London & Leicester etc. Tel: 08457 484950.

BUSES - Tel: 0870 608 2 608. Useful links for towpathers with Foxton, Husbands Bosworth, Welford and Kibworth Beauchamp.

MEANDERING through The Shires, and faithful to the 345 feet contour between Foxton bottom and Kibworth top, the Leicester Section continues to be self-effacingly shy, seemingly intent on avoiding all contact with civilisation. The nearest shops (including fish & chips) are to be found at Fleckney, a brisk walk across the fields from Bridge 73.

The unusual existence of a winding hole on the towpath side at DEBDALE WHARF recalls that this was the southern terminus of the canal for a dozen years during which fresh capital was raised.

The landscape hereabouts seems prone to instability. There was a spectacular breach at SMEETON in 1917. The local farmer's barley crop was ruined, both by the tidal wave of escaping water and the subsequent flood of sightseers. The embankment was rebuilt once again as recently as 1993.

SADDINGTON TUNNEL is said to be occupied by bats, though we didn't disturb any, perhaps by virtue of being bats enough already. The horse path runs enjoyably between hawthorn hedges across the top past spoil tips from the tunnel's excavation. KIBWORTH TOP LOCK marks the beginning of the canal's descent into the Soar Valley.

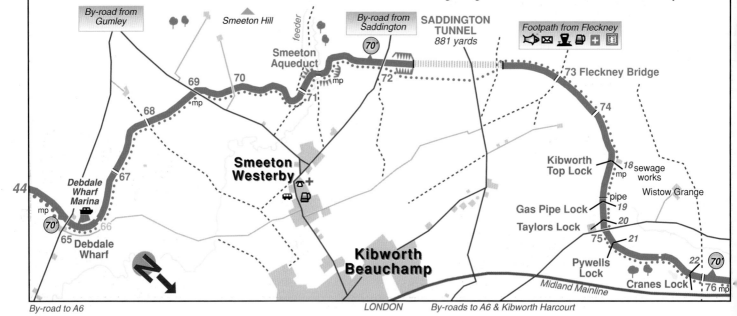

SHARING the journey with the River Sence and the Midland Main Line, the canal continues its descent to (or ascent from) Leicester through a succession of widebeam locks.

Throughout this section the countryside remains charmingly unspoilt - a refreshing change for southbound travellers after the urbanisation of Leicester.

The widebeam locks seem infuriatingly slow in equating their levels. Just when you think the gates are ready to be opened, a few more minutes have to pass. But the scenery has its compensations: some pretty churches (in the canalside graveyard at Newton there's a memorial in the form of a model church to an 8 year old boy), the Sence's attendant water meadows and peacefully wooded glades. By Bridge 86 are the remains of some flooded-out lime pits. At KILBY BRIDGE British Waterways offer pump-out and shower facilities. DOUBLE RAIL LOCK is crossed by a public footpath. It got its second set of safety rails following the drowning of an old lady.

Summary of Facilities

The main attraction along this length of canal is WISTOW RURAL CENTRE (Tel: 0116 259 2009) with its delightful model village (featuring some fairly intimidating-looking locks!), refreshments, craft shops, collectibles etc. Access from bridges 78 & 80. There are no shops on this section and just one pub, THE NAVIGATION, at Kilby Bridge (No.87). Tel: 0116 288 2280.

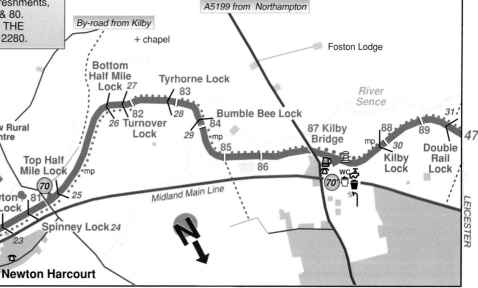

By-road from Kilby
+ chapel

A5199 from Northampton

Foston Lodge

Bottom Half Mile Lock 27

Tyrhorne Lock 83

River Sence

By-roads from Fleckney

26 Turnover Lock 82 28

Bumble Bee Lock

84

31

Wistow Hall   Wistow Rural Centre

29   mp

87 Kilby Bridge   88   89   47

85

Top Half Mile Lock   mp   30   Double Rail Lock

Sence Aqueduct   70   25   86   Kilby Lock

Newton Top Lock   81

77   Spinney Lock 24   Midland Main Line   70'

78   80   wc

79   23   N

Newton Harcourt

By-road to A6 and Great Glen   By-road to Wigston   A5199 to Leicester

LEICESTER

79

KEEPING to the flood plains of the Sence and the Soar, the Grand Union Canal makes its way into (and out of) Leicester largely unmolested by the urbanisation surrounding it. Only for a mile or two in the vicinity of South Wigston and Glen Parva do roads and housing mar the rural idyll. But there is so much to see and admire that it would be churlish to

grumble about such things. Sixty years or so ago, in *Narrow Boat*, L.T.C. Rolt averred that the 'sixteen miles of canal from Foxton to Aylestone...had little to commend them'. He and Angela were particularly dismayed by the 'monster gin-palace' at Blaby Bridge (No.98) and would no doubt feel vindicated to see it derelict now. Blaby Wharf once belonged to Pickfords. In latter years it has been a boatyard, but now is closed. Similarly defunct are the Midland Counties (Rugby-Leicester) and Great Central railways, though both have been transformed into public footpaths and cycleways. By Gee's Lock the River Soar introduces itself to northbound travellers. It rises in the vicinity of Watling Street south of Hinckley. Kings Lock (named not after royalty but a former lock-keeper) has retained its keeper's cottage. Whitewashed now, its lends the lock, charmingly located in a water meadow setting, considerable appeal. By Bridge 105 a 15th century packhorse bridge spans the Soar. It was once used as a route for carrying coal mined at Swannington into Leicester. Between Bridge 105 and the still intact girder span of the Great Central Railway, the Soar enters the canal, marking this as its highest navigable reach. At Bridge 106 stood Aylestone boathouse where skiffs and punts could be hired for many years.

The threat of vandalis has brought abo *locking* of the lock on the southern outskirts of Leiceste Boat crews need to equ themselves with at least on BW Watermate key to gain access to the paddle gear these locks. The locks are n 'family' friendly. The gates a heavy and access to the ot side is difficult even though hand rails are provided. Below KINGS LOCK the River Soar enters the cana beware strong currents aft rainfall.

YOU can tell a good deal about the character of a city by its attitude to the inland waterway on its doorstep. Leicester may yet lack the panache of Birmingham, but at least it is favourably disposed towards the navigation which defines the western rim of the city centre, and expends a good deal of care and concern on its upkeep and appearance.

WEST BRIDGE is the pivotal point of the waterway's eventful passage through Leicester. It was just to the north of here (in 1794) that the Union Navigation (to the south) and the Leicester Navigation (to the north) met at a point still recalled by a boundary stone on the towpath's edge. To the south of West Bridge lies MILE STRAIGHT, an impressive stretch of urban navigation spanned by handsome bridges and overlooked by a number of fascinating buildings from various periods in Leicester's history. Bede Island, a parcel of land squeezed between the original, and now un-navigable course of the Soar, and the so-called New Cut of 1890, dug to control flooding, has been redeveloped to bring new life and vigour to a rather decayed corner of the city once occupied by the Great Central Railway's goods yard and engine shed. West Bridge itself is framed by some attractive flats, converted from

a former hosiery mill, and Leicester's historic castle mound located in a pleasant little garden. Here a mooring pontoon (made secure by a locked gate accessed by BW's Watermate key) provides comfortable short-stay facilities for passing boaters - something that Leicester has traditionally lacked. In the gardens there's a statue of Richard III who spent his penultimate night on this earth in Leicester, and whose body was brought back here from Bosworth Field and displayed (naked and covered in blood) for the entertainment of the local populace.

And so, whichever direction you're travelling in, there's much more to see as what became the Grand Union journeys through Leicester, part river part canal. Several weirs demand care and attention, that by FREEMAN'S MEADOW LOCK being the

continued on page 82

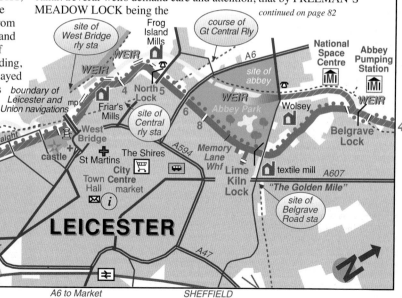

continued from page 81

fiercest by virtue of its great width. The old Midland Railway line to Burton-on-Trent spans the head of the lock on a redbrick viaduct, whilst the Great Central's engine shed stood alongside - this was *Flying Scotsman's* home depot in 1951, from where it would have worked Great Central line expresses south to Marylebone and north to Manchester via Sheffield. Below the weir, on the opposite bank of the river, and beyond the site of Leicester's electricity generating plant (where the poor used to fish for lumps of coal spilt from discharging barges) stands Leicester City Football Club's Walker Stadium which derives its name not, as traditionally, from the street which leads to it, or the neighbourhood of its location, but, as is the way of the football world now, from the name of its sponsor, the manufacturer of potato crisp based snacks.

ST MARY'S MILL LOCK is surrounded by bosky backwaters (one of which introduces the waters of the little known River Biam to the Soar) and presided over by a handsome eponymous mill building. A stone's throw away lies the gasworks and its unusual museum. Various cargoes of chemicals and gas waste were brought here by boat from Belgrave Gas Works on the far side of Leicester. In 1939 Tom and Angela Rolt moored *Cressy* by AYLESTONE MILL LOCK and caught the tram into the city centre.

Downstream from West Bridge the waterside is dominated by Friar's Mills, a handsome redbrick building with a belfry and golden ibex weather vane. Dating from the mid-18th century, it's thought to be Leicester's oldest factory, and belonged for many years to Donisthorpes, wool and cotton manufacturers. Either side of Soar Island lie Evans' and Hitchcock's weirs, both of which should be steered away from, especially when the draw is strong after bouts of rain. Soar Lane Bridge (No.4) - an elegant metal structure - dates from 1876 and was built to carry a railway line. Beside it an enigmatic piece of upended track is all that remains of a vertical lift bridge designed by Robert Stephenson to carry the Leicester & Swannington Railway in 1832.

Beyond Hitchcock's Weir the river and the canal lose sight of each other, and in doing so create Frog Island. Images of lily pads and a croaking chorus are dispelled by a galaxy of tall textile mills and sundry other factory premises which overlook NORTH LOCK. There may well, however, be frogs in the purlieus of Abbey Park with its boating lake, miniature railway

Friar's Mills, Leicester

Belgrave Lock, Leicester

and bandstand, a typical Victorian municipal park. In contrast, dyeworks proliferate on the opposite bank, bordering the A6's lugubrious route across the northern fringe of the city. This was Leicester's 'Wharf Street' neighbourhood where the "policemen walked the beat in pairs" for their own safety. Joseph Carey Merrick - 'the Elephant Man' - was born in nearby Lee Street in 1862. His name came, not so much from his looks, but from the fact that his mother had been crushed by a menagerie elephant during her maternity. Merrick died at the age of twenty-eight, after an adult life travelling in freak shows, breaking his neck by lying his weighty head on a bed unsupported by a pillow.

Leicester's main canal wharves were located hereabouts. It seems apt that the main wharf was known as Memory Lane, for, naturally, commercial trade can barely be remembered. Apart from one good-looking warehouse, the basins are rather dissolute now and not a place most pleasure boaters would care to linger. Probably the last cargoes to be unloaded here were consignments of timber imported via Wisbech and carried by the Seymour-Roseblade Company to Leicester via the River Nene in 1963.

On the far side of the Fosse Way stood the Great Northern Railway's impressive, but underused, terminus known as Belgrave Road. The last trains left in 1962, excursions for Skegness and Mablethorpe, Lincolnshire resorts favoured by generations of Leicester folk. It bears remembering that the whole concept of railway excursions emanated from Leicester when, in 1841, a certain Thomas Cook organised a Temperance outing from Leicester to Loughborough. It cost a shilling and was effectively the world's first package tour, including refreshments and entertainment by a brass band.

Wolsey's underwear factory was derelict and due to be redeveloped when we last passed through. At the head of BELGRAVE LOCK the towpath changes sides and the Soar returns. This backwater is navigable with diligence as far as the tail of a weir in Abbey Park, a delightful detour, but not one for novices. On the way you pass the National Space Centre looming surreally over the water before finding yourself in amongst a sargasso sea of water lilies and the glorious setting of a vibrant municipal park. It crosses your mind that this would be a wonderful setting for visitor moorings, but in reality the only place to tie up is a rather disconsolate jetty, an idea before its time perhaps.

Leicester (Map 48)

One of Britain's ten largest cities, Leicester, as the 'cester' part of its name implies, was a Roman settlement, known as Ratae, which prospered where the Fosse Way crossed the River Soar. Tangible remains of the Roman occupation survive in the Jewry Wall. Subsequent layers of history interweave and overlap in a city which, along with East Midland rivals Derby and Nottingham, came to symbolise the explosive growth of textile manufacturing in the 19th century. If Derby was silk and Nottingham lace, then Leicester was more practically based on hard-wearing worsted. The manufacture of footwear also became a significant part of the local economy. In 1936 a League of Nations report cited Leicester as the second most prosperous city in the world - The Hague in Holland was first! New life blood poured into Leicester in the Sixties and Seventies as its textile traditions attracted immigrants from the West Indies and East Africa, bringing to the city an especially vibrant Asian community. Likewise, Leicester avoided any symptoms of post-industrial malaise and now thrives as a centre of education as well as modern manufacturing and commerce.

MRS BRIDGES - Loseby Lane. Timeless tearooms. Tel: 0116 262 3131.
THE OPERA HOUSE - Guildhall Lane. Award-winning restaurant near St Martin's Cathedral. Tel: 0116 223 6666.
LE BISTROT PIERRE - Millstone Lane. French restaurant. Tel: 0116 262 7927.
THE CASE - Hotel Street. Stylish first floor restaurant overlooking 'The Cank', a meeting place for Leicester's gossip mongers since 1313. Tel: 0116 251 7675.
GIUSEPPES - Westbridge Close. Italian restaurant with riverside views opposite the Castle Visitor Moorings. Tel: 0116 251 8251.

TRAINS - Midland Mainline services to/from the North and London. Central Trains run along the Soar Valley in handy stages for towpath walkers. Tel: 08457 484950.
BUSES - services throughout the region. Tel: 0870 608 2 608.

Leicester claims to have Europe's largest covered market. At its edge look out for Walkers shop where the firm best known nationwide for its crisps sell an altogether more sophisticated selection of their pies. Elsewhere The Shires houses all the well known chain stores, whilst St Martins Square is a more discrete zone of designer outlets. In the northern suburb of Belgrave are many shops specialising in Asian foods and fashions.

TOURIST INFORMATION - Town Hall Square. Tel: 0906 294 1113
www.goleicestershire.com
ABBEY PUMPING STATION - Corporation Road. Tel: 0116 299 5111. Open daily. Preserved Victorian sewage pumping station whose Gimson beam engine is steamed on special occasions. Free admission, interactive toilet!
NATIONAL SPACE CENTRE - Exploration Drive. Tel: 0870 607 7223. Leicester's answer to Cape Kennedy - you have lift-off!
NEW WALK MUSEUM & ART GALLERY - New Walk. Tel: 0116 225 4900. Art & history combined, fine collection of German Expressionist works. Open daily, free admission. Well worth visiting for the building itself designed by Hansom of 'hansom cab' fame and to see New Walk, an extraordinary 18th century traffic-free thoroughfare a mile long.
LEICESTER BIKE PARK - cycle hire from office in Town Hall, only £4 for half a day.
NEWARKE HOUSES MUSEUM - The Newarke. Tel: 0116 225 4980. Reconstructed street scenes and the clothing of Britain's heaviest man. Open daily, admission free.
GAS MUSEUM - Aylestone Road. Tel: 0116 250 3190. Open Tue, Wed & Thur afternoons, admission free.
JEWRY WALL MUSEUM - St Nicholas Circle. Tel: 0116 225 4971. Roman remains. Open daily, admission free.

NORTH of Leicester the Soar Valley is riddled with gravel workings. Riddled rather than scarred, because the flooded gravel pits have been imaginatively incorporated into the Watermead Country Park, a green lung for Leicester folk, be they birdwatchers, windsurfers, dinghy sailors, ramblers, cyclists, anglers or sundry other categories of enthusiast not so easily classified. So commerce returns, in time, to nature, though a certain amount of gravel extraction continues, some of which was carried, until comparatively recently, a short distance along the Soar in widebeam pans pushed by diminutive tugs. Thurcaston Road Bridge (No.12) is an ancient mixture of brick and stone construction, part of which is said to date back as far as 1357.

Between Thurmaston and Cossington locks, the Soar goes off in a sulk, leaving the navigation to pursue a man-made cut and a short section of the River Wreake. Apparently the 18th century owners of Wanlip Hall didn't want dirty barges and even dirtier bargees spoiling their view and had the clout to have the navigation moved out of sight and mind. The Wreake had its own navigable history, once forming a liquid link with Melton Mowbray (presumably for the carriage of pork pies) and Oakham. The confluence of the Wreake and the Soar takes place immediately upstream of Cossington Lock.

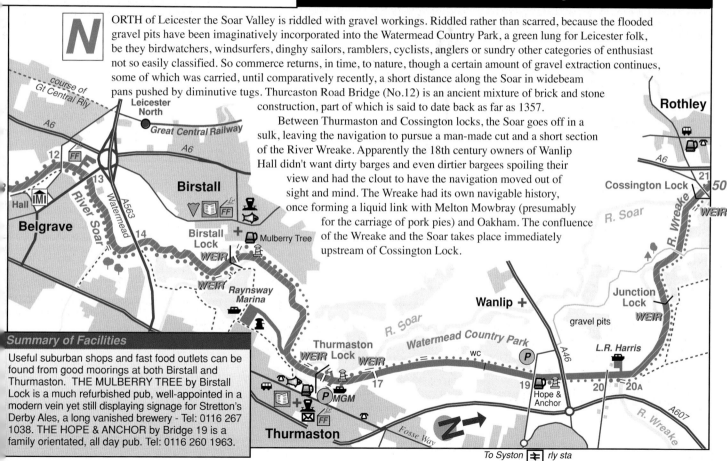

Summary of Facilities

Useful suburban shops and fast food outlets can be found from good moorings at both Birstall and Thurmaston. THE MULBERRY TREE by Birstall Lock is a much refurbished pub, well-appointed in a modern vein yet still displaying signage for Stretton's Derby Ales, a long vanished brewery - Tel: 0116 267 1038. THE HOPE & ANCHOR by Bridge 19 is a family orientated, all day pub. Tel: 0116 260 1963.

THIS is a particularly beautiful stretch of the River Soar, and one busy with boats too, given the existence of boatyards at Sileby and Barrow. To the west the landscape rises abruptly from the Soar Valley to the heights of Charnwood Forest, over eight hundred feet above sea level at its highest point and made up of volcanoes which last erupted a little matter of seven hundred million years ago. To the east the countryside rises less pyrotechnically in the direction of Leicestershire's Wolds.

The river and the navigation continue to enjoy a love-hate relationship, coming together then splitting up again, sometimes briefly as at Appleyard Island, often more extensively as at Mountsorrel and Quorn. At SILEBY LOCK there's a pretty brick-built mill, originally used for grinding corn, but in latter years, prior to its closure in the 1930s, owned by a firm making leather board for Leicester's shoe industry. Across the fields an old chimney marks the existence of a former brewery and maltings.

MOUNTSORREL has been a quarrying centre for many years, the local granite being ubiquitously used for kerb and paving stones. Hardwearing and pinkish in colour, they were once carried far and wide by water transport. In 1860 a massive railway bridge was built to capture much of the navigation's transport monopoly. Nowadays the stone goes over to the railway sidings and screening plants at Barrow by conveyor.

Nearing BARROW-UPON-SOAR, the river cascades over a sizeable weir and makes its way round to Quorn past the site of a former gypsum mill. The navigation channel assumes all the characteristics of a canal, passing the charming and much photographed Navigation Inn, and reaching BARROW DEEP LOCK which has a fall of 9ft 7ins and a set of colour light signals which turn red when the current in the river precludes safe boating.

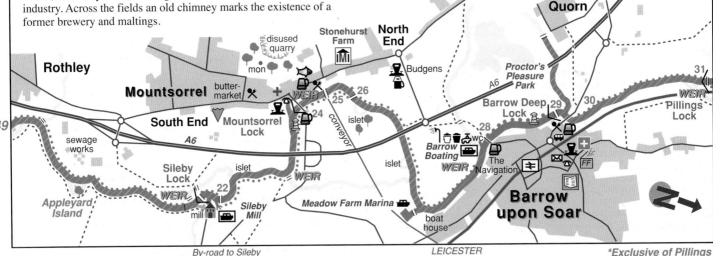

*Exclusive of Pillings

Barrow has the air of a small resort. The island formed by the canal cut and the river is occupied by Proctor's Pleasure Park - faintly old fashioned but still popular. PILLINGS LOCK is usually chained open throughout the summer months. It derives its name from a 19th century lock-keeper. The lock-cottage was demolished in 1957. At this point the Soar goes off (through a flood control gate and across a weir) on a long, un-navigable ramble to the east, thus avoiding Loughborough.

Rothley (Map 49)

The centre of Rothley village is about a mile west of Cossington Lock, and Rothley station on the preserved Great Central Railway is the best part of two miles from the Soar. Distance notwithstanding, you may find the walk worthwhile, for the village is well equipped with facilities: a fish & chip shop, newsagent, chemist, post office, general store and pubs. A stone pillar in the grounds of Rothley Court (now an English Inns hotel - Tel: 0116 237 4141) commemorates the site of William Wilberforce's draft plan for the abolition of slavery in the British Empire.

Sileby (Map 50)

Typical of the Soar Valley's industrialised villages, Sileby was a hosiery, and footwear centre, a sort of miniature 'Leicester'. It lies a pleasant quarter of an hour's walk from Sileby Mill and amongst its useful facilities are a Co-op store, NatWest bank, chemist, bakery, butcher, newsagent, Chinese takeaway, Indian and English restaurants, railway station and fish & chip shop.

Mountsorrel (Map 50)

The new course of the A6 has left 'Mount-Soar-Hill' dreaming sleepily of its busier past, not that you can saunter along the main thoroughfare without still paying some attention to the traffic. Notable structures are the old buttermarket dating from 1793, and Mountsorrel Hall, an Adam style pile on the corner of the old A6 and Sileby Lane. A hilltop memorial recalls the existence of a castle built here in the 11th century to guard over the valley's trade routes. Henry III had it demolished following a siege in 1217.

WATERSIDE INN - adjacent Mountsorrel Lock. Tel: 0116 230 2758. Everards pub offering lunches and dinners.
THE SWAN - Loughborough Road. Tel: 0116 230 2340. Its charming garden runs down to the weir stream. Inside the bar is stone-flagged and the imaginative menu is freshly-cooked to order.
THE BRIDGES BAR - Loughborough Road. Indian restaurant. Tel: 0116

230 4455. Mooring pontoon for customers.
Elsewhere in the village there are more pubs, a cafe by the buttermarket and a good fish & chip shop. Shops, at least within comfortable carrying distance of the river, are restricted to a small general store cum off licence.

i STONEHURST - Bold Lane, Mountsorrel. Tel: 01509 413216. Open daily, admission charge. "Family Farm & Museum". Fresh produce, gifts and refreshments. Access from Mountsorrel Lock - about 10 minutes walk. Great fun here: the highlight being a ride on a trailer hauled by a tractor up past the quarries into the brackeny hills.

Barrow upon Soar (Map 50)

A limestone quarrying village until 1910, Barrow is a village of fossils, by which we mean ancient remains of prehistoric animals as opposed to the present inhabitants - but there again...! Anyway one of the traffic roundabouts features a replica amphibious reptile known to its friends as an ichthyosaurus tenuirostris or plesiosaurus. Locals know it more simply as the 'giant kipper'.

THE NAVIGATION - canalside Bridge 28. Dates from 1794, photogenic exterior with waterside patio, convivial interior adorned with old river views. Good choice of pub food and real ales. Tel: 01509 412842.
THE BENGAL - adjacent Deep Lock. Balti restaurant. Tel: 01509 621000.
RIVERSIDE - canalside Bridge 30. Pizza & pasta restaurant and bars. Tel: 01509 412260.
SOAR BRIDGE - adjacent Deep Lock. Everards local. Bar food. Tel: 01509 412686. Fish & chips (Tel: 01509 414004) and take-aways in village.

Shops in the village centre (about six minutes from the lock) include a Somerfield supermarket, chemist, butcher, baker, grocer, newsagent, and post office.

TRAINS - useful stopping service linking Barrow with Loughborough and Leicester. Tel: 08457 484950.
BUSES - as above, but slower! Tel: 0870 608 2 608.

THE Soar Navigation reached Loughborough from the Trent in 1778 and immediately increased the town's prosperity beyond its promoters' wildest dreams - at one time it was paying its shareholders 150% dividends. The terminal wharf witnessed considerable scenes of commerce, redoubled with the arrival in 1794 of the Leicester Navigation and its tramway extension up on to the quarried heights of Charnwood. Not that many boaters see the site of the wharf, for it lies a few hundred yards beyond the dog-leg junction of the Leicester and Soar navigations at CHAIN BRIDGE, so called because a chain was strung across it when the toll keeper was off duty to prevent boatmen passing through without payment. A new mooring pontoon was in place on the wharf arm when we researched this guide, and new housing looked as if it would help to revitalise a hitherto seedy neighbourhood.

The Grand Union's passage through Loughborough is far from dull, being presided over by some interesting specimens of industrial archaeology, crane works, textile mills and neat little housing zones of varying antiquity. Bridge 35 is barely a few hundred yards away from the Great Central Railway's lovingly restored Central station, from which steam-hauled trains regularly recreate the atmosphere of a by-gone age. Ambitious proposals have been aired to extend their operation northwards to the outskirts of Nottingham along the former main line which crosses the canal on Bridge 37.

Either side of the town, the navigation traverses pleasant countryside. To the south it skirts the once marshy expanse of Loughborough Moors, passing the Peter Le Marchant Trust Centre founded in 1975 to give canal boating experience to the disabled - keep an eye out for its widebeam boats *Serenade* and *Symphony*, welcome reminders that this is, after all, a widebeam waterway all the way from the Trent to Market Harborough. North of Loughborough, once it has escaped the tentacles of sewage works and industrial estates, the navigation rejoins the Soar beyond BISHOP MEADOW LOCK where water, sewage and refuse disposal facilities are to be had.

Between here and the Trent the river forms the boundary of Leicestershire with Nottinghamshire.

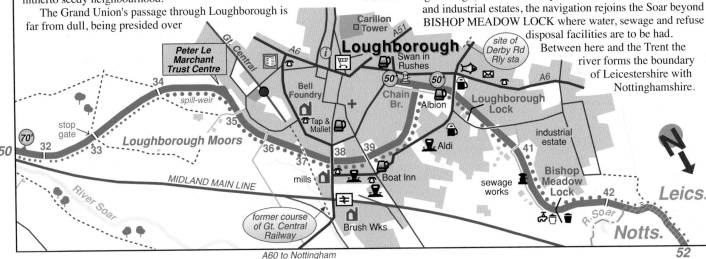

Loughborough *(Map 51)*

'Luff-burr-a' (and not 'Lug-bo-rug' as some visitors have been heard to pronounce it) is best known for its bell-making, diesel locomotive manufacture, and the sporting excellence of its colleges and University. Other famous businesses include Ladybird Books and 3M pharmaceuticals, but despite such overtones of industry, and a population not far off fifty thousand souls, the town centre has the charm of a modest country town, especially on Thursdays and Saturdays when the market's in full swing. We were particularly enamoured with Queens Park and its unusual 150ft high Carillon Tower and Church Gate, a narrow street of offbeat little shops.

BOAT INN - canalside Bridge 39. Popular, refurbished Marston's pub. Tel: 01509 214578.

ALBION INN - canalside near Chain Bridge. Unspoilt little pub with canalside patio and aviary. Interesting beers and bar meals. Tel: 01509 213952.

SWAN IN THE RUSHES - on A6 adjacent old wharf. Unprepossessing exterior transcended by good food, wide choice of beer and admirable absence of muzak. Accommodation. Tel: 01509 217014.

TAP & MALLET - Nottingham Road. Tel: 01509 210028. A beer-lover's pub, offering an ever varying range of unusual brews.

OLD MANOR HOTEL - Sparrow Hill. Tel: 01509 211228. Restaurant of smart hotel open to non-residents at the top end of Church Gate.

Good shopping facilities centred on the market place overlooked by a handsome town hall. Retail markets on Thursdays and Saturdays, Farmers Market on the second Wednesday of each month. Antiquarian bookshop on Church Gate - Tel: 01509 269860.

TOURIST INFORMATION - Town Hall. Tel: 01509 218113 *www.goleicestershire.com*

BELL FOUNDRY MUSEUM - Freehold Street. Tel: 01509 233414. Working foundry where 'Great Paul' was cast for St Paul's Cathedral in 1881. Open Tue-Sat.

CARILLON - Queens Park. Tintinnabulistic memorial to Loughbough's First World War dead dating from 1923. Regular 47 bell recitals throughout the summer and small military museum. Viewing balcony at top of tower. Open Easter to September afternoons only. Tel: 01509 263370.

CHARNWOOD MUSEUM - Granby Street. Tel: 01509 233754. Local history.

GREAT CENTRAL RAILWAY - Central Station (close to Bridge 35). Restored and mostly steam operated line offering 16 mile round trip to Leicester north and back. Large locomotives, long trains and stretches of double-track re-create a main line railway atmosphere. Gift shop and refreshment room on station. Operates Sat & Suns all year round together with weekdays during the summer. Wine & dine trains on Wed & Sat evenings. Tel: 01509 230726.

TRAINS - Midland Main Line and Central Trains services from Midland Station adjacent Bridge 38. Tel: 08457 484950.

BUSES - services throughout the area by Arriva, Kinch etc. Tel: 0870 608 2 608.

Zouch *(Map 52)*

ROSE & CROWN - pleasant waterside pub offering bar or restaurant food. Moorings for patrons and a play area in the garden for children. Tel: 01509 842240.

Kegworth *(Map 52)*

Busy village straddling the A6 notable for the tall spire of its church.

CAP & STOCKING - Borough Street. A worthwhile ten minute walk from moorings by Kegworth Shallow Lock. The pub's plain brick exterior belies the charm of its bars, one of which features stuffed birds and fish in glass cases - always a good sign! Out at the back there's a peaceful walled garden. No piped music, Bass from the jug and a simple menu of well cooked food. Tel: 01509 674814.

THE OTTER - riverside 1 mile south of Kegworth. Refurbished pub on the A6. Food & family orientated. Customer moorings. Tel: 01509 672245.

THE ANCHOR - adjacent Shallow Lock. Homely mock Tudor local. Food usually available. Tel: 01509 672722.

The village centre also offers a restaurant, Chinese and fish & chips.

Good range of shops in the centre, albeit 15 minutes from the river. Co-op store open daily 8-10 (8pm on Suns), chemist, newsagent and post office.

KEGWORTH MUSEUM - High Street. Open Wed & Sun afts Apr-Sep. Excellent little museum devoted to local history. Tel: 01509 673620.

O NCE you've inoculated yourself against the contagious rash of electricity pylons which stalk the Soar Valley, the landscape becomes utterly charming. Save for the short cut at 'Zotch', the Grand Union's course is quintessentially riverine and up there with the Nenes and Avons of this waterways world. Little wonder, then, that the Soar Boating Club, formed in 1953 after a round of drinks at the White House Inn (now The Otter) at Kegworth, but based at Normanton since 1961, should be such a flourishing organisation.

NORMANTON-ON-SOAR is beguilingly beautiful; but then, of course, you'd expect Pearsons to say that of anywhere with a ferry. This one is chain worked by Mr & Mrs Liddington from their pretty cottage at the southern end of the village and costs 25p per person, per passage; a negligible sum

for the fun to be derived from using it. We crossed on it one balmy July evening and picnicked in a harvested cornfield on the far bank.

The Zouch Cut by-passes a mill now converted but once used for the grinding of gypsum. The resultant powder went by water to Birmingham for paper-making. Oh the romance of it all! Between Zouch and Kegworth the river runs parallel to the A6. Hard to imagine when this was the most expedient road from London to the Lake District. Tongue Island was formed when a bend in the river was straightened out in 1826. Beside KEGWORTH DEEP LOCK lie the remains of an earlier chamber by-passed as part of a flood protection programme. Kegworth Road Bridge (No.45) is a graceful structure dating from 1785. The adjacent Shallow Lock is usually chained open between April and September.

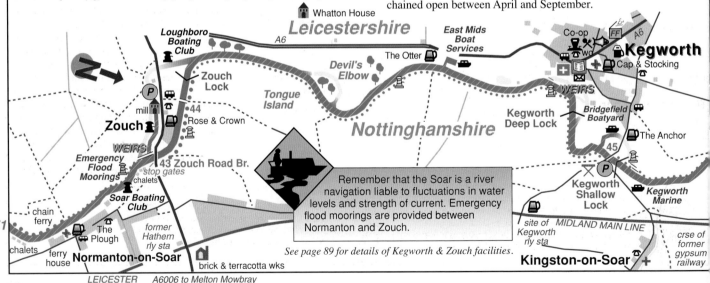

Remember that the Soar is a river navigation liable to fluctuations in water levels and strength of current. Emergency flood moorings are provided between Normanton and Zouch.

See page 89 for details of Kegworth & Zouch facilities.

*T*WENTY-FIVE miles downstream from Leicester, where it first becomes navigable, the River Soar has its confluence with the Trent overlooked by the eight, 300ft high cooling towers of Ratcliffe power station. It has packed a great deal into that short journey, and downstream travellers will be sorry to see it go. RATCLIFFE LOCK is another with a replacement chamber.

Reed-fringed and framed by flat fields, the Soar reaches REDHILL, a busy boating centre. In summer the lock is apt to be chained open.

The adjacent railway line tunnels through a wooded hillside, the northern portals being impressively rusticated. "Is that a castle?" someone asked. "No it's a railway tunnel!" Apart from the railway's huge box girders, there's no bridge across the Trent. In the old days boat horses were ferried across the river to reach the far towpath. Goodbye old Soar, when we think of you our spirits live up to your name!

The counties of Derbyshire, Leicestershire and Nottinghamshire meet at TRENT LOCK and you have a choice of routes : east to Nottingham, north along the Erewash Canal, or west to Shardlow and the Trent & Mersey. On this map we assume you're making for the latter along the broad and often windswept reach to Sawley. Pleasure boats and sailing dinghies scuttle about providing an obstacle course for ponderous canal craft. A goods railway spans the tail of SAWLEY LOCKS which are automated and duplicated. *Pearson's South Midlands Canal Companion* takes up coverage west of Sawley, and used in conjunction with this guide provides full coverage of the East Midlands Ring.

Map labels:

To Shardlow

Sawley Bridge Marina

Sawley Locks (duplicated & mechanised)

Derbys.

R. Trent

freight only

To Ilkeston & Langley Mill

Mills

Trent Lock

EREWASH CANAL

Leics.

A453 from M1 (Jnct 24)

Ratcliffe Lock

Redhill Lock

sailing club

R. Soar

WEIR 46

WEIR 47

The Steamboat Tea Rooms

Ratcliffe-on-Soar

WEIR

Notts.

Ratcliffe Power Station

Redhill Marina

WEIR

flood-gates

CRANFLEET

MIDLAND MAIN LINE

R. Trent

To Nottingham

At the confluence of the Soar and the Trent take special care to avoid the draw towards Thrumpton's massive weir, even though it's protected by a boom. The best policy is to keep close to the west or south bank of the Trent at this point.

Walkers from the Trent to the Soar and vice versa are faced with a lengthy detour via field paths and tracks between Sawley and Redhill - refer to OS Landranger Map 129.

Hire Bases

ALVECHURCH BOAT CENTRES - Gayton Marina, Northampton Arm, Map 19A. Tel: 08708 35 25 25. www.alvechurch.com

BARROW BOATING - Barrow-on-Soar, River Soar, Map 50. Tel: 01509 415001.

BLISWORTH TUNNEL BOATS - Blisworth, Grand Union Canal, Map 20. Tel: 01604 858868.www.canalcraft.com

CANALBOAT HOLIDAYS - Weedon, Grand Union Canal, Map 18. Tel: 01327 340739. www.canalboat-holidays.com

CLIFTON CRUISERS - Clifton Wharf, Oxford Canal, Map 4. Tel: 01788 543570. www.cliftoncruisers.com

CLUB LINE CRUISERS - Swan Lane Wharf, Coventry, Map 1. Tel: 024 7625 8864. www.swanlanewharf.co.uk

COLLEGE CRUISERS - Combe Road, Oxford, Map 16. Tel: 01865 554343. www.collegecruisers.com

CORONET CANAL CARRYING - Wilton Marina, Grand Union Canal, Map 17. Tel: 01327 844442. www.coronetcanal.co.uk

FOXTON BOAT SERVICES - Foxton, Leicester Section, Map 4?. Tel: 0116 279 2285. www.foxtonboats.co.uk

GREBE CANAL CRUISES - Pitstone Wharf, Grand Union Canal, Map 27. Tel: 01296 661920.

NAPTON NARROWBOATS - Napton, Oxford Canal, Map 7. Tel: 01926 813644. www.napton-marina.co.uk

OXFORDSHIRE NARROWBOATS - Lower Heyford, Oxford Canal, Map 13. Tel: 01869 340348. www.oxfordshire-narrowboats.co.uk

ROSE NARROWBOATS - Stretton-under-Fosse, Oxford Canal, Map 2. Tel: 01788 832449.www.rose-narrowboats.co.uk

SILEBY MILL - Sileby, River Soar, Map 50. Tel: 01509 813583. www.silebymill.co.uk

UNION CANAL CARRIERS - Braunston, Grand Union Canal, Map 6. Tel: 01788 890784. www.unioncanalcarriers.co.uk

VIKING AFLOAT - Rugby, Oxford Canal, Map 4. Tel: 01905 610660. www.viking-afloat.com

WELTONFIELD NARROWBOATS - Welton, Grand Union Canal, Map 17. Tel: 01327 842282. www.weltonfield.co.uk

WILLOW WREN - Rugby, Oxford Canal, Map 4. Tel: 01788 562183. www.willowwren.co.uk

WYVERN SHIPPING - Linslade, Grand Union Canal, Map 26. Tel: 01525 372355. www.canalholidays.co.uk

Day Boat Hire

BARROW BOATING - Barrow-on-Soar, River Soar, Map 50. Tel: 01509 415001.

BLISWORTH TUNNEL BOATS - Blisworth, Grand Union, Map 20. Tel: 01604 858868.

COLLEGE CRUISERS - Oxford, Oxford Canal, Map 16. Tel: 01865 554343.

DENHAM DAY BOATS - Denham, Grand Union Canal, Map 34. Tel: 01895 271070.

FOXTON BOAT SERVICES - Foxton, Leicester Section, Map 44. Tel: 0116 279 2285.

GREBE CANAL CRUISES - Pitstone Wharf, Grand Union Canal, Map 27. Tel: 01296 661920.

KILWORTH WHARF - North Kilworth, Leicester Section, Map 42. Tel: 01858 880484.

MK AFLOAT - Milton Keynes, Grand Union, Map 23. Tel: 07721 025325.

LEIGHTON LADY - Leighton Buzzard, Grand Union, Map 26. Tel: 01525 384563.

OXFORDSHIRE NARROWBOATS - Lower Heyford, Oxford Canal, Map 13. Tel: 01869 340348.

ROSE NARROWBOATS - Stretton-under-Fosse, Oxford Canal, Map 2. Tel: 01788 832449.

SILEBY MILL - Sileby, River Soar, Map 50. Tel: 01509 813583.

STOKE BRUERNE BOAT CO - Stoke Bruerne, Grand Union, Map 20. Tel: 01604 862107.

TOOLEY'S BOATYARD - Banbury, Oxford Canal, Map 10. Tel: 01295 272917.

UNION WHARF NARROWBOATS - Market Harborough, Leicester Section, Map 44. Tel: 01858 432123.

Boatyards

ASPLEY MARINA - Aspley, Grand Union Canal, Map 31. Tel: 01895 449851

AYNHO DOCK - Aynho Wharf, Oxford Canal, Map 12. Tel: 01869 338483.

BARROW BOATING - Barrow-on-Soar, River Soar, Map 50. Tel: 01509 415001.

BLISWORTH TUNNEL BOATS - Blisworth, Grand Union Canal, Map 20. Tel: 01604 858868.

BLUE HAVEN MARINE - Crick Wharf, Oxford Canal, Map 5. Tel: 01788 540149.

BRAUNSTON MARINA - Braunston, Grand Union Canal, Map 6. Tel: 01788 891373.

BULBOURNE DRYDOCK - Bulbourne, Grand Union Canal, Map 28. Tel: 01442 822256.

CALCUTT BOATS - Southam, Grand Union Canal, Map 7. Tel: 01926 813757.

CANALBOAT HOLIDAYS - Weedon, Grand Union Canal, Map 18. Tel: 01327 340739.

CLIFTON CRUISERS - Clifton Wharf, Oxford Canal, Map 4. Tel: 01788 543570.

CLUB LINE CRUISERS - Swan Lane Wharf, Coventry, Map 1. Tel: 024 7625 8864.

COLLEGE CRUISERS - Combe Road, Oxford, Map 16. Tel: 01865 554343.

COSGROVE MARINA - Cosgrove, Grand Union Canal, Map 22. Tel: 01908 562467.

BATES BOATYARD - Aylesbury Arm, Map 28A. Tel: 01296 632017.

COWROAST MARINA - Cowroast, Grand Union Canal, Map 29. Tel: 01442 823222.

CRICK MARINA - Crick, Leicester Section, Map 41. Tel: 01327 860640.

DEBDALE WHARF - Kibworth, Leicester Section. Map 45. Tel: 0116 279 3034.

DENHAM MARINA - Uxbridge, Grand Union Canal, Map 34. Tel: 01895 239811.

FENNY MARINA - Fenny Compton, Oxford Canal, Map 8. Tel: 01295 770461.

FOXTON BOAT SERVICES - Foxton, Leicester Section, Map 44. Tel: 0116 279 2285.

GRAND JUNCTION BOAT CO - Gayton Junction, GUC, Map 19. Tel: 01604 858043.

GREBE CANAL CRUISES - Pitstone Wharf, Grand Union Canal, Map 27. Tel: 01296 661920.

HAREFIELD MARINA - Harefield, Grand Union Canal, Map 33. Tel: 01895 822036.

HEYFORD WHARF - Lower Heyford, Oxford Canal, Map 13. Tel: 01869 340348.

HIGH LINE YACHTING - Iver, Slough Arm, Map 35A. Tel: 01753 651496. Northolt, Paddington Arm, Map 38. Tel: 01753 651496.

HILLMORTON BOAT SERVICES - Hillmorton, Oxford Canal, Map 4. Tel: 01788 578661.

KILWORTH WHARF - Kilworth, Leicester Section, Map 42. Tel: 01858 880484.

KINGFISHER MARINA - Yardley Gobion, Grand Union Canal Map 21. Tel: 01908 542293.

KINGSGROUND NARROWBOATS - Enslow, Oxford Canal, Map 14. Tel: 01869 351321.

MEADOW FARM MARINA - Barrow, River Soar, Map 50. Tel: 01509 812215.

MGM BOATS - Thurmaston, River Soar, Map 49. Tel: 0116 264 0009.

MIDDX & HERTS BOAT SERVICES - Winkwell, Grand Union Canal, Map 30. Tel:01442 872985.

MILLAR MARINE - Stowe Hill, Grand Union Canal, Map 18. Tel: 01327 349188.

MILTON KEYNES MARINA - Milton Keynes, Grand Union Canal, Map 23. Tel: 01908 672672.

NAPTON NARROWBOATS - Napton, Oxford Canal, Map 7. Tel: 01926 813644.

OXFORDSHIRE NARROWBOATS - Heyford, Oxford Canal, Map 13. Tel: 01869 340348.

PACKET BOAT MARINA - Cowley Peachey, Grand Union Canal, Map 35. Tel: 01753 651496.

ROSE NARROWBOATS - Stretton-under-Fosse, Oxford Canal, Map 2. Tel: 01788 832449.

SILEBY MILL - Sileby, River Soar, Map 50. Tel: 01509 813583.

SOVEREIGN WHARF - Banbury, Oxford Canal, Map 10. Tel: 01295 275657.

SPL MARINE - Brentford, Grand Union Canal, Map 37. Tel: 020 8560 9326.

TOOLEY'S BOATYARD - Banbury, Oxford Canal, Map 10. Tel: 01295 272917.

UNION CANAL CARRIERS - Braunston, Grand Union Canal, Map 6. Tel: 01788 890784.

UNION WHARF NARROWBOATS - Market Harborough, Leicester Section, Map 44. Tel: 01858 432123.

UXBRIDGE BOAT CENTRE - Uxbridge, Grand Union Canal, Map 34. Tel: 01895 252019.

VIKING AFLOAT - Rugby, Oxford Canal, Map 4. Tel: 01905 610660.

WELFORD MARINA - Welford, Leicester Section, Map 42. Tel: 01858 575995.

WELTONFIELD NARROWBOATS - Welton, Grand Union Canal, Map 17. Tel: 01327 842282.

WHILTON MARINA - Whilton, Northants, Grand Union Canal, Map 17. Tel: 01327 842577.

WILLOWBRIDGE MARINA - Stoke Hammond, Grand Union Canal, Map 24. Tel: 01908 643242.

WILLOWTREE MARINA - Paddington Arm, Map 36. Tel: 020 8841 6585.

WILLOW WREN - Rugby, Oxford Canal, Map 4. Tel: 01788 562183.

WYVERN SHIPPING - Linslade, Grand Union Canal, Map 26. Tel: 01525 372355.

T.F. YATES - Newbold, Oxford Canal, Map 3. Tel: 01788 569140.

How To Use The Maps

There are fifty-six numbered maps whose layout is shown by the Route Planner inside the front cover. Maps 1 to 16 cover the Oxford Canal between Hawkesbury, on the outskirts of Coventry, and Oxford where there is a link to the Thames. Maps 17 to 39 cover the Grand Union Canal between Braunston and Brentford and Paddington. Maps 40 to 53 cover the Leicester Section of the Grand Union between Norton Junction and Trent Lock. The maps are easily read in either direction. The simplest way of progressing from map to map is to proceed to the next map numbered from the edge of the map you are on. Figures quoted at the top of each map refer to distance per map, locks per map and average cruising time. An alternative indication of timings from centre to centre can be found on the Route Planner. Obviously, cruising times vary with the nature of your boat and the number of crew at your disposal, so quoted times should be taken only as an estimate. Neither do times quoted take into account any delays which might occur at lock flights in high season.

Using The Text

Each map is accompanied by a route commentary. Details of settlements passed through are given together with itemised or summarised information on facilities. Regular readers will already be familiar with our somewhat irreverent approach. But we 'tell it as we find it', in the belief that the users of this guide will find this attitude more valuable than a strict towing of the tourist publicity line.

Towpath Walking

The simplest way to go canal exploring is on foot. It costs largely nothing and you are free to concentrate on the passing scene; something that boaters are not always at liberty to do. Both the Oxford and Grand Union (Main Line) canals are now recognised as long distance footpaths in their own right. As usual the maps show the quality of the towpath, and whilst it does vary from area to area, none of it should prove problematical for anyone innured to the vicissitudes of country walking. We recommend the use of public transport to facilitate 'one-way' itineraries but stress the advisability of checking up to date details on the numbers quoted.

Towpath Cycling

At present it is necessary for cyclists wishing to use towpaths to acquire a free of charge permit from a British Waterways office - see opposite.

Boating

Boating on inland waterways is an established, though relatively small, facet of the UK holiday industry. There are over 30,000 privately owned boats registered on the canals, but in addition to these numerous firms offer boats for hire. These range from small operators with half a dozen boats to sizeable fleets run by companies with several bases.

Most hire craft have all the creature comforts you are likely to expect. In the excitement of planning a boating holiday you may give scant thought to the contents of your hire boat, but at the end of a hard day's boating such matters take on more significance, and a well equipped, comfortable boat, large enough to accommodate your crew with something to spare, can make the difference between a good holiday and an indifferent one.

Traditionally, hire boats are booked out by the week or fortnight, though many firms now offer more flexible short breaks or extended weeks. All reputable hire firms give newcomers tuition in boat handling and lock working, and first-timers soon find themselves adapting to the pace of things 'on the cut'.

Navigational Advice

LOCKS are part of the charm of canal cruising, but they are potentially dangerous environments for children, pets and careless adults. Use of them should be methodical and unhurried, whilst special care should be exercised in rain, frost and snow when slippery hazards abound. We lack space for detailed instructions on lock operation: trusting that if you own your own boat you will, by definition, already be experienced in canal cruising; whilst first-time hire boaters should be given tuition in the operation of locks before they set out.

On the Oxford Canal, Northampton and Aylesbury arms and Leicester section at Watford and Foxton, the locks are of the standard narrow variety; but on the GRAND UNION main line the locks are widebeam and capable of accepting two narrowboats side by side. Turbulence can be a problem when travelling uphill in wide locks, especially if your boat is the only vessel in the lock at the time. A rope cast around the lockside bollards will usually solve this. You might also benefit from opening the paddle on the same side as your boat first, this tends to hold the boat against the lock wall and prevent it from crashing about as the water floods in.

LIFT BRIDGES are a feature of the OXFORD CANAL but the majority of them remain open to boats except when being used by local farmers to gain access to their fields on the far bank. The moral is to 'leave them as you find them' - the bridges, that is, not the farmers.

MOORING on the canals featured in this guide is per usual practice - ie on the towpath side, away from sharp bends, bridge-holes and narrows. An 'open' bollard symbol represents visitor mooring sites; either as designated specifically by British Waterways or, in some cases, as recommended by our personal experience. Of course, one of the great joys of canal boating has always been the ability to moor wherever (sensibly) you like. In recent years, however, it has become obvious, particularly in urban areas, that there are an increasing number of undesirable locations where mooring is not to be recommended for fear of vandalism, theft or abuse. It would be nice if local authorities would be prepared to provide pleasant, secure, overnight facilities for passing boaters who, after all, bring the commerce of tourism in their wake.

CLOSURES (or 'stoppages' in canal parlance) traditionally occur on the inland waterways between November and April, during which time most of the heavy maintenance work is

undertaken. Occasionally, however, an emergency stoppage, or perhaps water restriction, may be imposed at short notice, closing part of the route you intend to use. Up to date details are usually available from hire bases. Alternatively, British Waterways provide a recorded message for private boaters on 01923 201402. Stoppages are also listed on BW's web site at www.britishwaterways.co.uk

TIDAL THAMES - Should you intend joining the River Thames at Brentford (not an excercise for beginners to undertake) you should seek advice from the Port of London Authority on 020 7265 2656 and ensure that you passage through Thames Lock is booked in advance - Tel: 020 8560 1120.

Emergencies
British Waterways operate a central emergency telephone service: Tel: 0800 4799 947.

British Waterways

British Waterways
South East Waterways
Witan Gate House
Milton Keynes
MK9 1BW
Tel: 01908 302500.

British Waterways
London Canals
Sheldon Square
Paddington Central
London
W2 6TT
Tel: 020 7985 7200

British Waterways
Mather Road
Newark
Nottingham shire
NG24 1FB
Tel: 01636 704481.

Trip Boats
CANAL CRUISES - Regent's Canal, Paddington, Map 39. Tel: 020 7485 4433.
COSGROVE NARROWBOATS - Grand Union Canal, Cosgrove, Map 22. Tel: 01525 372853.
FOXTON BOAT SERVICES - Leicester Section, Foxton, Map 44. Tel: 0116 279 2285.
GREBE CANAL CRUISES - Grand Union, Pitstone, Map 27. Tel: 01296 661920.
INDIAN CHIEF - Grand Union, Stoke Bruerne, Map 20. Tel: 01604 862428.
JASON'S TRIP - Regent's Canal, Paddington, Map 39. Tel: 020 7286 3428.
LEIGHTON LADY - Grand Union, Leighton Buzzard, Map 26. Tel: 01525 384563.
LINDA CRUISING CO - Grand Union, Milton Keynes, Map 23. Tel: 07973 915652.
LONDON WATERBUS CO - Regent's Canal, Paddington, Map 39. Tel: 020 7482 2550.
WALKER'S FERRY - Grand Union, Rickmansworth, Map 33. Tel: 01923 778382.

Societies
The Inland Waterways Association was founded in 1946 to campaign for retention of the canal system. Many routes now open to pleasure boaters may not have been so but for this organisation. Membership details may be obtained from: Inland Waterways Association, PO Box 114, Rickmansworth WD3 1ZY. Tel: 01923 711114. Fax: 01923 897000.

Acknowledgements
Thanks to: Brian Collings for the signwritten cover; David & Jennifer Alison for boating & hospitality, Toby Bryant & family for regular updates, Karen Tanguy for proofs and transport and Giampiero Lo Giudice and all at STIGE for production.